RADICALTHREAD.

Edited by Lesley Millar

EXHIBITING MEMBERS

HONORARY MEMBERS (EXHIBITING)

HONORARY MEMBERS (NON EXHIBITING)

Morag Gilbart
Jennifer Gray
Margaret Hall-Townley
Jennifer Harris
June Hill
Jan King
Janet Ledsham
Alison Liley (Mrs Erridge)
Barbara Marriott
Professor Lesley Millar MBE
Professor Anne Morrell
Linda Parry
Hannah Frew Paterson MBE DA
Sue Prichard
Andrew Salmon
Diana Springall
Barbara Taylor

FRIENDS

Miranda Brookes
Maria Theresa Fernandez
Heather Martin
Lesley Mitchison
Irene Ord
Barbara Siedlecka
Isabel Wright

HISTORY OF THE 62 GROUP

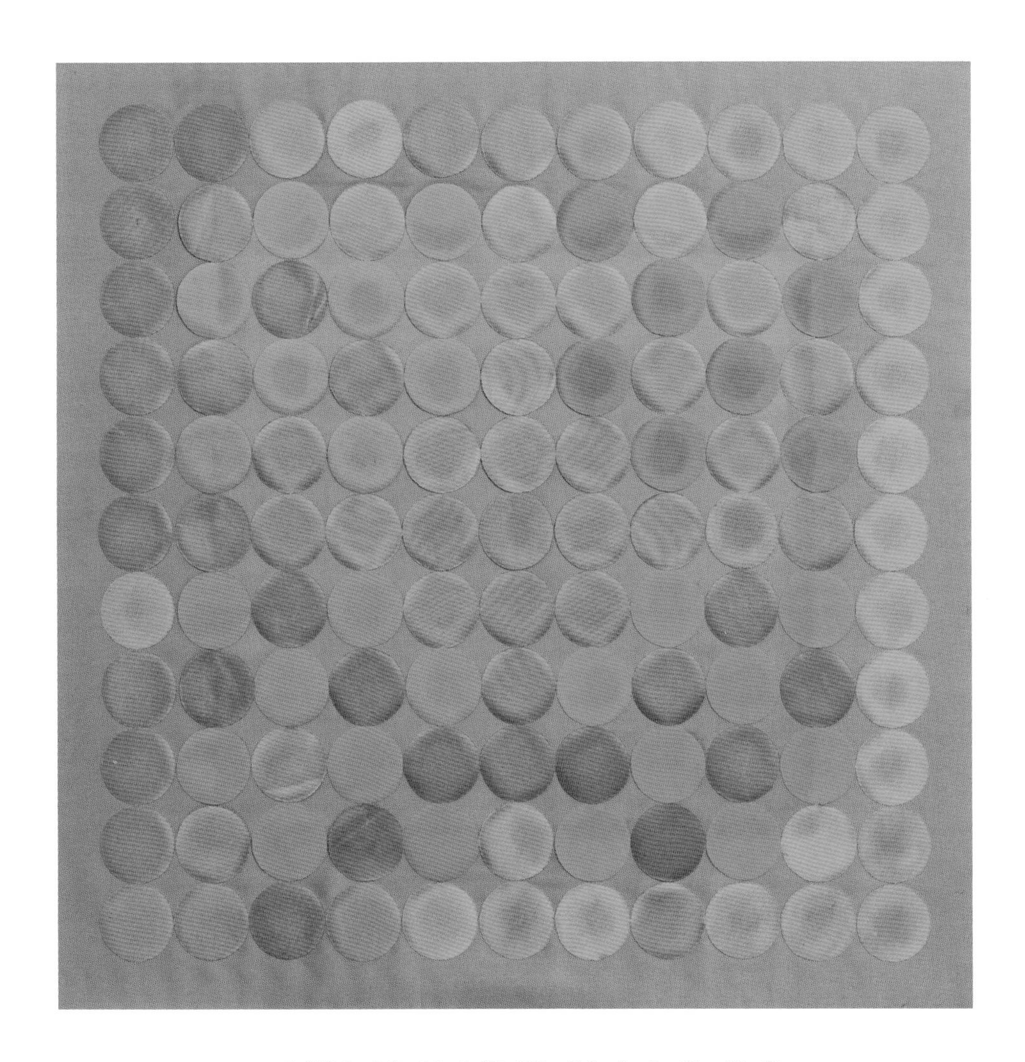

JENNY GRAY. 1966

THE 62 GROUP of TEXTILE ARTISTS

A history of the first 50 years 1962 - 2012

With contributions from founder members - Alison Erridge (nee Liley) and Jennifer Gray, both Chairmen in the early years and with extracts from a conversation between Jae Maries (current Chairperson), Jan Beaney (member since 1963) and Audrey Walker (member since 1967).

In the late 1950's Alison Erridge (nee Liley), Jennifer Gray and Joy Clucas, teachers of embroidery in the National Diploma of Design (NDD) were greatly concerned about the professional prospects for their talented students after graduation. The opportunities to exhibit their work and to have it valued alongside their peers in other disciplines were bleak.

Jenny Gray: Alison Erridge, Joy Clucas and I wanted to make a difference in people's attitude to embroidery which was considered to be ... the poor relation of Textiles and certainly Fine Art. I suppose we wanted to share our excitement with fabrics, stitching, textiles and colour ..... and expose this fresh vision to a wider public. At the time there was no outlet for the newly qualified embroiderers to exhibit. ......There seemed a tremendous need to 'upgrade the image' by finding like-minded embroiderers from as many backgrounds as possible to meet, discuss and exhibit together. Alison Erridge was the prime mover of this.

They decided that collective initiatives would be stronger than individual efforts, perhaps a campaigning group could be formed? So they invited a wide range of embroidery teachers to come to a meeting in November 1962 at the Embroiderers' Guild in London.

Alison Erridge: I remember meeting Lady Hamilton Fairley and Miss Sinclair Salmon at the Embroiderers' Guild in Wimpole Street, London. We asked if we could meet (as a group) and exhibit there. They said 'yes' as long as we all became members of the Guild.

Jenny Gray: That first meeting was an eye opener! We came from all sorts of backgrounds, enthusiastic to see the possibilities of exhibiting together and prepared to work hard and endlessly to encourage new membership.

As well as Alison, Jenny and Joy, other people at the meeting included Audrey Tucker, Pat Scrase, Judy Barry and Marie Shawcross.

It was the formative, inaugural meeting of The 62 Group of Embroiderers. The formal connection with the Embroiderers' Guild had been established and at this first stage any embroiderer could become a member.

Very soon after the formation of the Group, in 1964 or 65, it was realised that 'open membership' had inherent problems. Work submitted for exhibitions could be very skillful but could equally be lacking design ability or creative content.

Selection for membership and for inclusion in exhibitions had to be agreed and, although it caused much upset at the time, it was a crucial decision. It was written into the Constitution and remains a fundamental principle of the Group to this day. This shift away from 'open membership' gave the Group a new title; The Professional Group of the Embroiderers' Guild.

Jan Beaney: I wasn't at that first meeting in November 1962 but joined three months later when the first exhibition was being discussed.

Audrey Walker: I visited that first exhibition and I remember its impact in the rather staid atmosphere of the Guild. It consisted mostly of small framed panels but the quality of the drawing, design and the subject matter was really remarkable.

Jan Beaney: The second show was in the following December - embroidered Christmas cards! We might cringe now but the concept was unusual at the time, lots of orange and pink colours, very 60's.

The next big step forward was taken when the Group was sponsored by the Art Exhibitions Bureau, an organisation which toured art exhibitions to venues such as public libraries, throughout the UK. The Group's new approach to embroidery reached a very wide public. It was a breakthrough and the work sold at a great pace which was a real encouragement supporting the members' belief that there was an appetite for change. The pressure to produce new work (replacing sold work) in time for the next venue, became a problem and so the touring ceased after about two years. However the Group was by then well known and respected for its professionalism and for the innovative nature of the work. Exhibitions in prestigious venues followed and due to the initiatives of Jan Beaney and Julia Caprara, 62 Group shows were held in London at the Royal Festival Hall (1967), the Victoria and Albert Museum (1970 and 72), the Commonwealth Institute (1972), TUC Congress House (1970 and 1972). A sustainable exhibition programme had been established.

From 1963 to 2011 no fewer than 85 exhibitions have been held, mostly in the UK but also in Japan, Israel and the Netherlands. All these have been organised voluntarily by the members of the Group and its committee, funded through the membership fees with occasional support from the Arts Council of England.

Over these 50 years there have been huge changes in the Textile Arts, not least in the breaking down of barriers between textile disciplines. College courses changed as students assumed the right to move across different areas and the 62 Group recognised that being described as an embroidery group had become limiting. Some twenty years after its foundation, the membership was opened up to makers from any textile medium. The formal link with the Embroiderers' Guild came to an end and the title changed to The 62 Group of Textile Artists.

Jan Beaney: One of the 62 Group's most important contributions to the development of Textile Art since 1962, has been through education. Many members have published books, they have run workshops, short courses and given lectures. It is doubtful that textiles would now be a subject in Art 'A' levels without members of the Group being in a position of influence in schools and colleges.

Jae Maries: Yes, education was a major objective when the Group was formed and we still offer educational events alongside most of our exhibitions.

Audrey Walker: The publication of 'Radical Thread' is a new aspect of the Group's educational programme, one which we hope will be of lasting value to students and teachers as well as to the wider public.

In the Group's 50 year, it has 57 exhibiting members, many of whom have international recognition for their textile work and their teaching. There are a further 25 Friends and Honorary Members, distinguished in the field of textiles. The number of Exhibiting Members has been fairly constant and is a manageable number for a group run voluntarily and without premises or administrative support.

Jan Beaney: The initial idea behind the formation the Group was that it would help young people leaving art college to exhibit their work. It was only meant to last for five years but when that time arrived, there was dismay at the thought of losing the Group. 'Where would our exhibiting opportunities come from?' And so we continued.

Audrey Walker: The Group is still keen to recruit recent graduates and to give them support when struggling to keep going in the tough 'real' world.

Jae Maries: These younger members are essential for the health and continuation of the Group. We mostly rely on our members teaching in colleges to encourage their students to find out more about the 62 Group and see the benefits for membership. They are our future.

In its 50th year, the 62 Group is proud of its record, but it is not complacent – there is much to be considered. Changes come thick and fast in new technologies and means of communication. Some textile courses have been closed or absorbed into more generalised qualifications so it is important now as it has ever been, that the distinctive nature, history and contemporary relevance of textiles is shown and understood.

Textiles can be found in almost all cultures. They celebrate, narrate and are part of everyday experience. This 'text', this 'voice' of textiles still needs to be heard and seen through exhibitions, publications and research. The 62 Group is one such voice and its founding objectives still hold:- to show strong, innovative work to the widest possible public through the continuing exploration of this most basic medium which touches us all. The 62 Group will continue to mount arresting exhibitions and to provide high quality textile teaching at all levels.

Today's members of the 62 Group of Textile Artists look forward to meeting the challenges and opportunities in the coming years.

Jan Beaney, Jae Maries, Audrey Walker.
September 2011

Radical: arising from or going to the root or source; (especially of change or action) relating to or affecting the fundamental nature of something; far-reaching or thorough: a radical overhaul of the existing regulatory framework.[1]

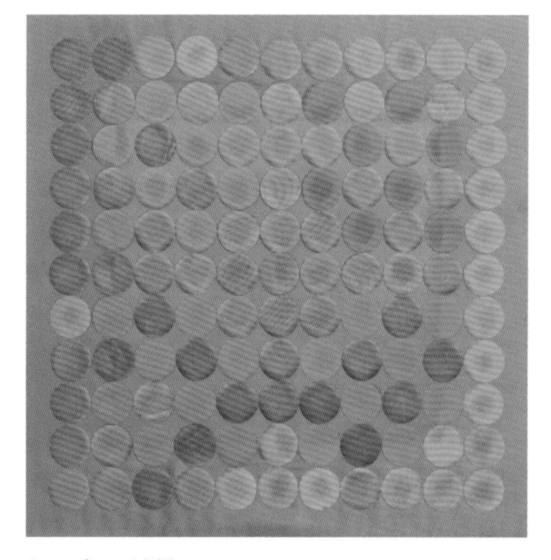

Jenny Gray, 1966

It is so hard, from where we are now, to think back to the position of Textile Art in the middle of the last century. Textile Art in the early sixties was in more or less the same position it had occupied pre-war. In the main, its position in terms of embroidery was placed within the ecclesiastical, and in terms of weaving: modern tapestries, designed mainly by painters and woven by anonymous artisans. As 62 Group Member and previous Chair, Audrey Walker, comments about the period: *'Where was the contemporary work in Britain? It seemed to be invisible.'* [2] And so in 1962 a group of embroiders decided to come to together as a pressure group and a support system, believing that collectively they might achieve a public profile where individually they might be struggling. A collective voice may be louder than a single one. This was the founding of the 62 Group, initially under the umbrella of the Embroiderers Guild, and then as an independent organisation.

These were women of amazing talent and strength of purpose. They were determined to place the best of textile art within the context of the best art practice, whilst never loosing sight of the high quality skills and material understanding that were at the root of their work. These standards have been the guiding principles for the Group since its formation and are applied with the same rigour today, and are probably the major reason for its longevity. There is a rolling exhibition programme and all members must submit their work for selection. Failure to submit or rejection of submitted work for three consecutive exhibitions and the membership is forfeit. This is a hard line to take, but it has ensured the maintenance of quality, the commitment of the members and relevance to contemporary ideas.

Back to the sixties and to the early days of trying to promote new and exciting Textile Art when no-one outside the field was interested, cracks in the edifice of fine art conventions were appearing. Elissa Auther in her book 'String, Felt and Thread' charts the process of the art world's assimilation of fibre and fibre's contribution to the history of art. She takes us from Eva Hesse's struggles with the male dominated, 'Greenbergian', American art world of the 1950's and early 60's through to context-led work by Elaine Reichell, Anne Wilson and Ghada Amer. [3]

Elsewhere in the world, the Lausanne Tapestry Biennale in 1962 began the promotion of contemporary tapestry and by 1971 it was moving textiles off the wall and into areas previously defined as the territory of sculpture. Japanese textile artists were demonstrating that traditional skills and material understanding could be used to create previously undreamed of contemporary responses to the space within the built environment. Textile artists in Eastern Europe were using textiles, which were considered Decorative Arts, to create subversive Textile Art that went unnoticed by the Soviet Union censors.

The period covered by the 62 Group coincides with this intense debate around the relative positions of craft and art, with textiles occupying a central position and textile artists choosing, at different times, to place their work within or outside the category. A survey of the labels assigned to textile art during this period demonstrates the to and fro: Decorative Artists, Fibre Artists, Designer Makers, Artists, Studio Practitioners... It is a debate which, as Audrey Walker commented in her Foreword to 'Stitched Textiles' in 1990: *'has merely led, time after time, to a re-inforcing of the privileged position of painting and a needlessly defensive position for textile work.'* In reaction textile artists stopped looking to define their work against other art forms, instead choosing to research, describe and celebrate the work for its own sake. This brought about the realisation that the resulting works need no justification as art or defence as craft, creating confidence in the place of the work within its own context and history.

Step by step, refusing to give up, the members of the 62 Group have infiltrated their work into the mainstream and made their presence felt. The record of exhibitions organised by the Group is exceptional and testament to the singularity of purpose of its members. However, organisations have to develop, to respond to changing attitudes, interests, possibilities. It is incumbent upon any art form to develop its own tensions, and that tensile nature provides much of its excitement and interest: a static art form is a dead art form. Textile art comes with its own inner tensions as a result of its *'undecidable'* [4] location and the 62 Group have responded to the 'new', broadening their constituency to include constructed textiles in all their many manifestations. However, rather than diffusing the energies inherent in the art form, this provides a continuing dynamic, a 'radical thread', derived from the movement between tradition and innovation.

ROOTS/ROUTES

It is these various journeys between tradition and innovation – the routes and roots of the members of the 62 Group – that I would like now to address. The strengths of the 62 Group lie in the similarities and the differences. The similarities are those drawn from textiles, the differences are in the outcomes. In thinking how to describe and understand the Group within the context of this book I felt it important to begin at the beginning – the beginning of each member's interest in cloth. The sheer number of members (57), some living outside the UK, rendered it impossible to visit and interview each and so I devised a questionnaire which was completed by all.

The 62 Group identifies itself as being one of textile artists and the questionnaire had a very particular focus: to identify the role of textiles in the development of the work of each of the artists. Firstly, to draw out personal memories and the importance of an involvement - or lack of it - in some aspect of textiles within the (extended) family. I also included questions about traditional practice and its role in the development of work. These questions could be categorised as the roots. Secondly, I was also interested in the routes taken by the members to their current ways of working. Whether a formal training in textiles had been involved or not, and how important it was for each that the work was recognised as having emerged from a textile route/root by the viewer. Thirdly, I asked for information about each member's involvement in the 62 Group and their thoughts about the Group.

Not surprisingly, the ways of answering these questions were as diverse as the ways in which the members approach their work. Responses varied from several thousands of words to single word answers. The integrity and honesty of the answers were extraordinary, and in many cases extremely moving; the themes that emerged were as strong and delicately precious as silk thread. The answers have been woven together by me, using the actual words, to create the individual narratives within the necessary word count of a maximum of 375. The texts were then sent back to the members who altered, deleted or added as each felt necessary. These final versions are the ones accompanying each member's images of work.

Although there are exceptions to all the threads I have drawn together in this introduction, in reading through the responses you will see that, by far and away, the most important influence has been the involvement with cloth in some way during childhood. This is unsurprising on one level, given the universality of cloth in our daily lives. However it is the centrality of the experience in its influence on later choices that is so marked. Growing up surrounded by textile involvement has been cited again and again: *'Within my family there was a definitely tradition of making things but it was more about necessity– doing it because we needed a dress or curtains. I knew about sewing and crochet in the same way as I knew about stringing beans and putting up shelves and in a way they have all remained as part of my artistic vocabulary.' (Louise Baldwin)*

The experiences vary from a general atmosphere of making: *'I come from a very creative background... my Mum always has an ongoing project, appliqué quilts or samplers; in his younger years my Dad repaired the sails on his round the world Yacht Race...' (Aimee Spilsted)* through to an intense hands-on involvement: *'I remember sewing at home with my mother, making embroidered binca mats and stitched kits...This kept me occupied for hours, totally absorbing me.' (Jane McKeating)*

Many of the members grew up with a family committed to, what we now call re-cycling, and in earlier days was understood as make do and mend: *'...my bare foot alighting from under my patchwork quilt, onto a pegged wool rug. It was made from unravelled woollen jumpers, so the crimp had a special feel between the toes.... The make do and mend/ thrift activity still exists within my practice.' (Jeanette Appleton)* Collars were turned, a piece of cloth during its lifespan could move from curtain to cushion to duster or soft toys; scraps were collected and used over and over. Clothes would be altered and moved down the sibling chain. *'My well-remembered 'new' skirt for school was made by Mum from a wool fabric – grey/green, thick, stiff and unbending in such a short length and with an unsettling diagonal – which today I recognise was once a cavalry twill overcoat.' (Jan Miller).*

The tools of making, particularly the sewing machine, occupied a central position in the house: *'My Mum made our clothes and I was always aware of the feel of the fabrics and the smell. I loved to see her open up the dining table and lay out the patterns and start to cut.' (Hilary Bower)* and *'The dining room carpet was her cutting table, and was a dangerous place to walk barefoot - continuously scattered with abandoned dressmaking pins.' (Heather Belcher)* That other staple of Homecraft, knitting, seemed always to be in progress. Throughout my childhood my grandmother patiently knitted mittens, which I constantly lost, from one year end to the next. The internal 'photograph' we carry of certain members of the extended family is inextricably bonded to an activity: *'I can never remember my paternal grandmother without knitting in her hands and the same with Aunt Kate and her crocheting.' (Amanda Clayton)*

However, not everyone was so happy to acquire the traditional skills: *'Felt is my 'rebellion' to the dressmaking RULES and perhaps to my mother.' (Heather Belcher)* Even to the extent of aversion: *'I remember being made to work a Union Jack Flag in chain stitch when I was about 6 and I loathed anything to do with stitch all through my school years!' (Jan Beaney)*

The work of many of the members is clearly identifiable as emerging from a textile root and one that is central to their practice: *'The work has its roots in textile history and practice, the language of cloth and stitch being the pivot, around which aspects of social history are expressed.' (Colette Dobson)* With some that root is less obvious, but still it is important for the artist that the viewer is aware: *'I realise that it is critical to my current work that there is a textile root and that it is visible to others, even in a simple, minimal way' (Hilary Bower)* and for others it is sufficient just that the textile root is there: *'I do feel all my work does have some sort of textile root, even the carved stone relief's and drawings, but it is not important to me that the viewer recognises this.' (Clyde Olliver)*

(1) Oxford Dictionary
(2) All quotations from 62 Group members, unless otherwise stated, are taken from their responses to the questionnaire, which accompanies the images of their work in this book.
(3) Elissa Auther. String, Felt, Thread: the hierarchy of art and craft in American art. Minnesota. University of Minnesota. 2009
(4) Sarat Maharaj 'Textile Art – Who Are You?' as reprinted in 'Reinventing Textiles Vol.2 Gender and Identity' Ed. J. Jeffries. Winchester. Telos Art Publishing. P8, 2001
(5) Jennifer Harris. Ourspace: tradition and innovation in contemporary British textile art in Cloth & Culture Now ed. L. Millar. Epsom. University for the Creative Arts.P147, 2007

ROUTES

The routes taken to their current practice have, in many cases been influenced by their close involvement with textiles while growing up, sometimes consciously: *'...the tradition of making had an impact on the choice I made when going to art college. Studying textiles felt like familiar territory.' (Elaine Megahey)*. And for some it was a moment of revelation: *'I first studied Fine Art painting and then went to Goldsmiths College to do a Postgraduate Diploma in Textile Art. My epiphany moment came as I sat at the machines with the realisation that thread had the potential to transport me anywhere and need have no function.' (Alice Kettle)*

However, certainly not all intended to use textiles or textile related techniques or ideas in their practice when they set out as artists. Yet it seems that deep familiarity with cloth eventually emerged in one form or another: *'Originally I trained as an oil painter... all those years of handling cloth and selecting fabrics left an indelible impression on me, so the decision to become involved with textiles later in my life, can be seen as a natural progression in my work.' (Jae Maries)* This sometimes happened despite intentions: *'Fortunately I was awarded scholarships which took me to Art Schools to study Painting. It never occurred to me that embroidery might be taken seriously as an art form. Then, by chance in 1960 I saw an exhibition of "fabric collages" by Margaret Kaye-I was entranced!' (Audrey Walker)*

Traditional practice is embedded in the approaches taken by the members to their work: *'I find many traditional textile practices command my interest; for the social and cultural practices embedded in the history of textile making and use, for the level of skill and knowledge of materials embodied in practice through design and production'. (Caroline Bartlett)* It is the sense of being part of a continuum, however radical the personal outcome might be, that underpins so much of the practice within the group: *'I love the long tradition of weaving and the suggestion that by weaving (and encouraging others towards weaving), I am a part of continuing that tradition. Weaving permeates so many avenues from technology, cultural traditions, language and mythology which for me, enriches the craft'. (Kay Smith)* The traditional influences range from the international: Navajo blankets, Peruvian back-strap weaving, embroideries from Gujarat, basket weavers in Alaska, New Zealand and Canada – the list goes on, to the local: Irish crochet work, Yorkshire rag rugs, braid making, button holes. However, the concern is not with reproducing that traditional practice but understanding and translating it into contemporary material responses to life as experienced now. *'I've always been interested in contested areas of textile practice, Embroidery, Pattern, Lace and recently Floral Textiles. I've pioneered new ways of researching and developing ideas sourced from Textile History.' (Michael Brennand-Wood)*

CONCLUSION

Textile Art provides has provided a counterpoint to the 'end of art' as heralded by Duchamp and the Ready Made: the beginning of approaches in which the artist searches for the unpredictable, often rejecting traditional skills as a means of achieving the outcome. The best of Textile Art emerges from highly skilled material and technical understanding, which is then translated into work that may sit within or outside of the current areas of discourse but which does satisfy the need for texture, narrative and the Haptic experience.

The 62 Group has acted as both a focus and a catalyst for change, radical change, in the perception and the actuality of contemporary textile art. Over and over members have underscored the importance of being in the company of their peers, the opportunities to discuss and compare ideas, to be valued and supported, and the sense of identity within the Group. For the future, the next 50 years, the hopes and aspirations as expressed by the members are for the Group to maintain that radical thread connecting the roots, routes and outcomes, *'thriving on the freedom found in the interstices between the two ideas of tradition and innovation'* [5]

Such a route requires courage and confidence and, as Rozanne Hawksley has written: *'Good luck and clear thinking to us all.'*

Lesley Millar
Professor of Textile Culture
University for the Creative Arts
December 2011

The making and embellishment of cloth permanently existed as an ordinary everyday occurrence throughout my childhood. The sewing machine and cloth, knitting needles and wool were constantly used to survive. The make do and mend/ thrift activity still exists within my practice. Inspired by my mother's amazing ability to teach herself fine knitting and sewing skills to create any shape. Inherent in the process of childhood discovery, I continue this inherited play with materials. Not afraid of mistakes or following a prescribed route, respecting and seeing the potential of materials.

JEANETTE APPLETON.

One specific memory which links with my current practice: my bare foot alighting from under my patchwork quilt, onto a pegged wool rug. It was made from unravelled woollen jumpers, so the crimp had a special feel between the toes. The image was of a lamb prancing in a meadow full of wild flowers. Drawn and pegged on sacking, my mother's childhood memories greeted me every morning. This detail of nature gave me a very early way of looking and continues in my soul. It was her escape into longing and nostalgia, from everyday practicalities. Watching her embroider delicate and perfect stitches into transfer printed crinoline ladies in front of thatched cottages and English herbaceous borders. This nostalgia of place and memory is a focus in my current practice, but towards tourism and ecological concerns.

Felt is the traditional textile practice that I find most inspirational. It was a very new form of cloth to be explored in a contemporary way and I was fortunate to be at the beginning of the new wave of interest. It has an immediacy, the moment you pull a piece of fibre, one can perceive this as drawing or painting. The weight and density, scale and form can be changed and manipulated during the process. The wonderful hidden magic in the scales of the wool can attach and transform other materials, giving them new meaning and associations.

I have been a member of the 62 Group for 17 years and during that time it has become more international and taken a wider view of what is textile art.

Title: Landline: Double Edged Encounters, 2003
Textile installation in the Sainsbury Centre, Norwich
Produced for 'Through The Surface: collaborating textile artists from the UK and Japan'. Purchased by the Contemporary Arts Society for the textile collection at Nottingham City Museum and Art Gallery
Size: 28.4 x 0.6 x 3.0 metres
Materials: Needle felt, heat transfer prints on fabric, machine embroidered labels. Dyed Merino wool, synthetic fabric/thread and metal rod/hooks
Photo: Pete Huggins

Title: Dry Drifting Shadows: Alpujarras, 2010
Size: 910 x 560 x 20 mm
Materials: Felted needle felt and stitch. Dyed merino wool tops and various natural fibres, fabrics and threads
Photo: Peter Stockdale

Within my family there was definitely a tradition of making things but it was more about necessity – doing it because we needed a dress or curtains. I knew about sewing and crochet in the same way as I knew about stringing beans and putting up shelves and in a way they have all remained as part of my artistic vocabulary.

I trained in embroidery at Goldsmiths college, it is the media I have become familiar with. It has a history for me. I'm drawn to the touch and the marks I can make; the way I can hold a piece of fabric or paper in my hand and put it up against another; the meeting of materials. I'm not sure if stitch is always crucial to the work itself but it is the way I find myself expressing ideas. It helps me clarify the image. Even now I don't feel technically accomplished and perhaps this is partly because I would prefer people see the work for the image it presents rather than the technique or media within which it is realized.

Title: Did we really? 2011 (right)
Size: 42 x 42 cm
Materials: Mixed fabrics with hand and machine stitch
Photo: David Ramkalawon

Title: Everything together. 2011(below)
Size: 39 x 40 cm
Materials: Mixed fabrics with hand and machine stitch
Photo: David Ramkalawon

LOUISE BALDWIN.

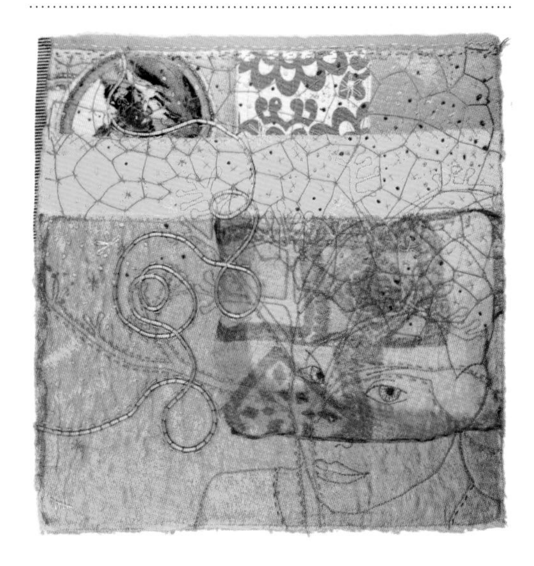

Mostly my work starts with some vague atmosphere, a colour in mind. It's not until later that I really know what I'm doing. I bring together pieces of fabric, paper, a drawing or a sentence, allowing things to move in an organic way. It's a slow and slightly unfocused start that involves lots of changes on route but things sharpen up towards the end when the imagery, ideas and composition gel. I don't always end up with what I think I'm going to and perhaps this is what keeps me going.

I find that I'm drawn to other artist's work that pulls together unexpected materials and images, making the extraordinary from the ordinary, more than anything I am excited by sculpture, installation and collage.

I have been a member of the 62 Group for over 30 years and have seen plenty of changes as we have grown in strength and professionalism. The support of the group as a whole and the ambition of individuals has kept us moving, by taking up new challenges and staying connected.

I remember the times, at the age of six, that I spent sitting with my mother, sewing tiny wrap-over vests (from brushed cotton I think) by hand for my sister who arrived one week before my seventh birthday. They were quiet, precious, memorable moments and there were many times like this afterwards. We didn't have a television, but we listened to the radio. My father was a farmer and not around a great deal during the day so I spent a lot of time with my mother and sister and we would sew. From those early days I became a serious stitcher, always making things and knitting too. I was content to experiment and sample stitch and construct all sorts of things made from material. I haven't stopped sewing since and it still excites me.

HELEN BANZHAF.

I trained and worked as a fashion designer for a short while following achieving my degree, but I was rather timid and I felt uncomfortable working in the fashion world. Once a year there would be at the ILEA, a recruitment session for prospective tutors for London Adult Education Institutes and inspectors in various disciplines would hover about identifying suitable tutors to appoint. The Home Economics Inspector approached me and asked if I'd ever considered teaching in a school needlework department. It had never crossed my mind but one week later I was in a classroom in south east London teaching needlework and although it was terrifying, I'd unexpectedly found my metier. I started making small tentative, non-functional machine embroidered pieces on my domestic sewing machine. As I have become more confident with my textile work over the years, I use abstract pattern. I see myself nowadays more as a fine artist and my stitches are worked like brush strokes.

I joined the 62 Group in 1997 because of its great reputation for diverse and innovative work. Over this time the boundaries have continued to be pushed with mixed media being a bigger feature of textile work and I hope it will never stand still.

Title: Untitled (above, and detail far right)
Size: 34 x 22 cm
Materials: mercerized cotton threads on calico
Photo: Michael Wicks

Title: Untitled from the Tumbling Leaves series (top)
Size: 28 x 19 cm
Materials: mercerised cotton threads on calico
Photo: Helen Banzhaf

Title: Untitled from the Fragments series (bottom)
Size: 17 x 12 cm
Materials: mercerized cotton threads on calico
Photo: Helen Banzhaf

I find many traditional textile practices command my interest; for the social and cultural practices embedded in the history of textile making and use, for the level of skill and knowledge of materials embodied in practice through design and production. Travel, in many parts of the world has been significant for me in developing an appreciation of the richness and breadth of textile culture, and techniques. One of my most enduring memories is of travelling alone through West Africa with a handful of pictures of indigo dyed cloths from the Beving Collection (British Museum). Showing these photos to local people sent me on a journey deep into Guinea and opened up a realisation as to just how 'social' these cloths were. These introductions to textiles around the world have had a profound effect in fostering my passion for textiles, but it has taken a long while to begin to contextualise these experiences in relation to my own practice.

CAROLINE BARTLETT.

Textile remains fundamental to my practice not only in substance but also for what it, and processes used on it, can suggest. However, whilst I define myself through textile work, it is unimportant that the viewer recognises my work as having a textile root. I like to work across a breadth of practice, switching between gallery based work and responses to site; historical, museological and archival. Working with collections has led me to explore how such knowledge systems represent and promote the construction of individual and collective identities, memories and value systems. Ideas of imprinting, erasing and reworking, drawn from my textile print background, have been consistent components in my work in terms of content, process, choice of, and response to project and site. This has found form for example, in imprinting the grass through the use of stencils and resist techniques to selectively stop grass from growing, or in allusions to fragility and elements being worn away, hidden or replaced.

I have been a member of the 62 Group since 1993. It provides me with a network of peers, exhibiting opportunities and an excellent arena to test ideas and take risks.

Title: Backwards, Forwards IV (1 of 8) (below)
Size: 34 x 72 cm
Materials: cotton thread, wool. Hand stitched
Photo: Caroline Bartlett

Title: Backwards, Forwards IV; detail (top left)
Title: Backwards, Forwards VI detail (top right)
Title: Surrogate III; detail (bottom left)
Title: Surrogate I; detail (bottom right)

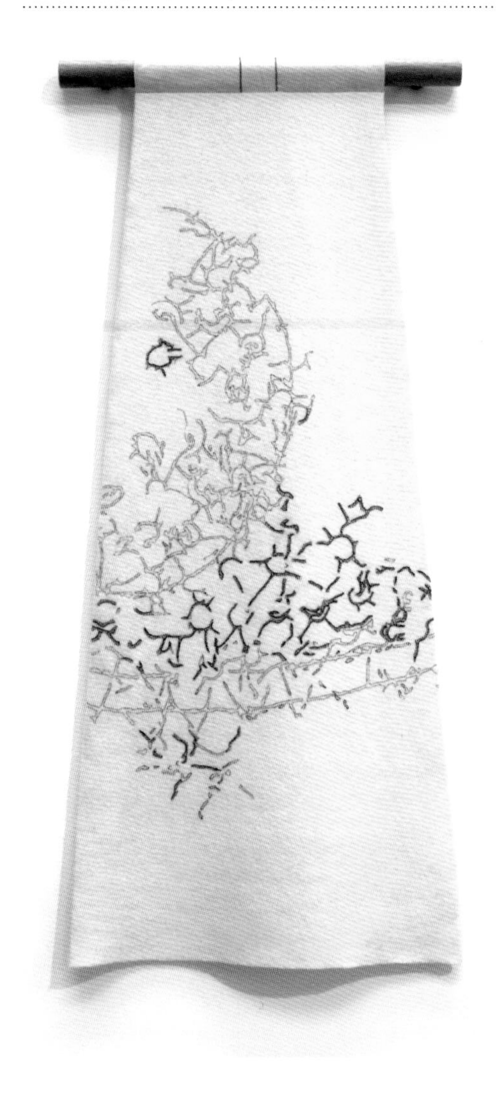

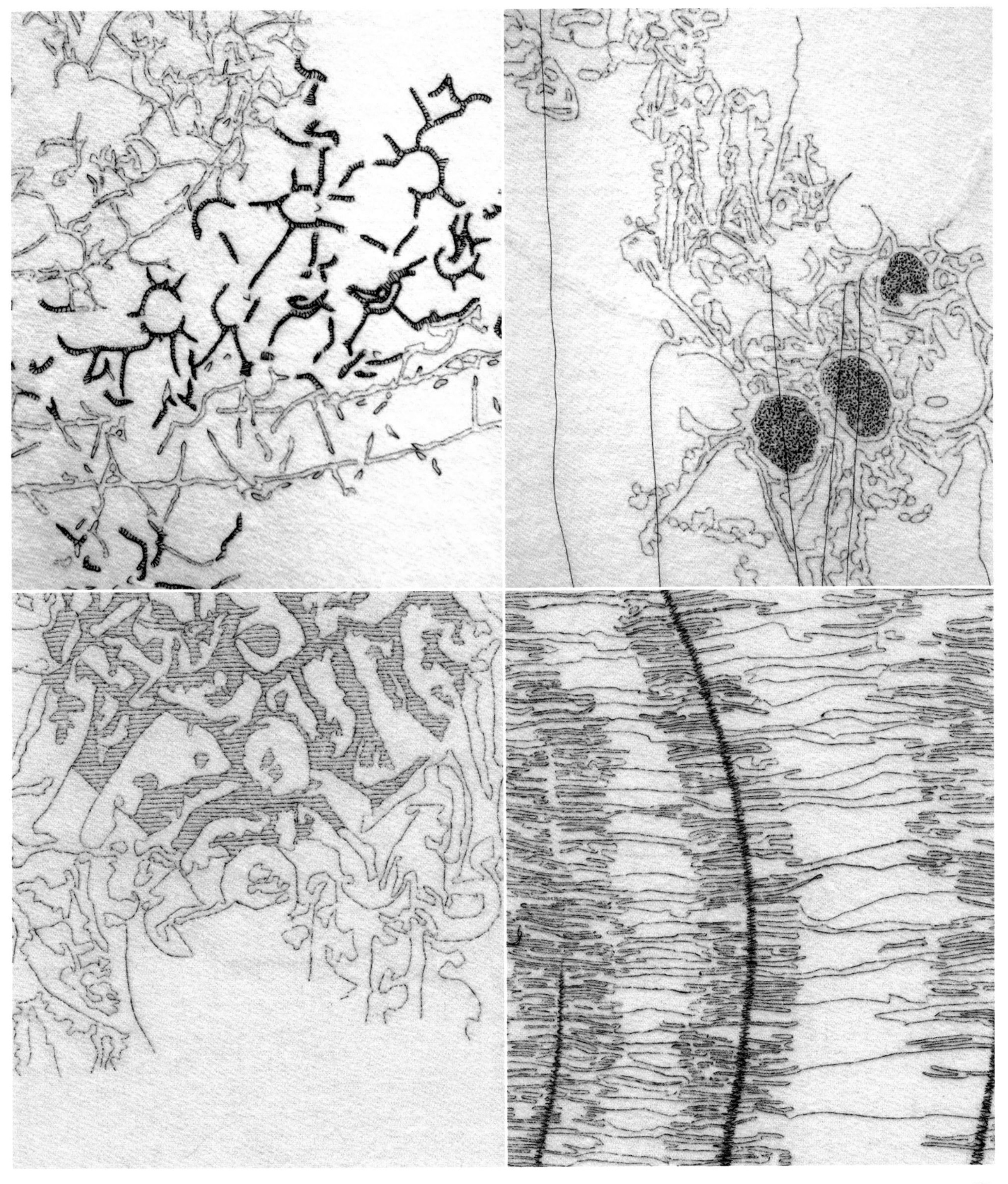

I remember being made to work a Union Jack flag in chain stitch when I was about 6 and I loathed anything to do with stitch all through my school years! My first teaching job involved teaching Art to A level and surprisingly, O level embroidery. I was one page ahead in Mary Thomas's Embroidery Book and Barbara Snook's History of English Embroidery. Total panic!!! Luckily, Eirian Short saved the day. I had spent a day a week with her in my final year at Hornsey College of Art where I had learned a few basic techniques. During my probation year I travelled across London every Wednesday evening to study for City and Guilds Embroidery. My awareness and respect for traditional textile disciplines developed over the three years I took to complete my additional qualifications. During this time, I visited the Embroiderers' Guild which led to my invitation to join the 62 Group and to write my first book.

JAN BEANEY.

At art school my painting practice involved a fascination with light on surfaces and technically the contrast between heavy textural work and the build up of glazes. However, the more I studied textiles, the more I realised the exciting range of possibilities available. Most importantly, I realised that a stitch could be viewed as a mark as with a pencil line or a brush stroke. Painting and drawing play a large part in informing my work. Landscape in all its forms continues to be totally absorbing and I endeavour to capture a memory or an essence of a place in a simple, understated manner. Constructing an appropriate fabric is then the challenge.

I joined the 62 Group in 1963, three months after its inception. Fifty years all but three months. Since then the Group has become independent, moving away from the Embroiderers' Guild umbrella. Selection has become more stringent and there is an acceptance of a wider range of textile disciplines. The Group has had a strong influence on the development of textiles as an art form due to exhibitions and publications and hopefully this will continue for many years to come.

Title: Skala Eressos: Early Evening (below and detail)
Size: 51 x 76 cm
Materials: Machine and hand stitching on soluble film to form a new cloth
Photo: Michael Wicks

My mother made almost all of my three siblings clothes and mine when we were children. She was an accomplished dressmaker, teaching dress making and tailoring in the local Adult Learners College. There was always at least one if not more garments under construction at any given time. The dining room carpet was her cutting table, and was a dangerous place to walk barefoot - continuously scattered with abandoned dressmaking pins. It was here that I learnt the complicated rules of cutting and constructing a garment; 'placing on the fold', 'cutting on the cross or bias', matching patterns or stripes on the seams and cutting the cloth as economically as possible.

HEATHERBELCHER.

I didn't make a conscious decision to work with textiles, I wanted to be an artist first and foremost but somehow the familiarity of fabric seeped in without me noticing. Just before I left Goldsmiths College, Mary Burkett, the then curator of Abbott Hall Museum Kendal, gave a talk about traditional felts from Central Asia. The very next day with only three months to go until my degree show, I set about teaching myself how to make felt, and this has been my area of specialism ever since.
Felt is my 'rebellion' to the dressmaking RULES and perhaps to my mother. Felt has no warp and no weft in its structure, it is simply a mass of tangled fibres. Pattern pieces need not be placed on the straight grain or bias of the cloth according to normal convention. Felt is sometimes referred to as an 'anti-fabric' because it is not constructed from a linear thread as is the definition of a textile. I enjoy this sense of being on the edge, or in the borderlands between one thing and another.

I joined the 62 Group in 2002 and I think it is important to include the widest spectrum of work as possible that is related to the processes and language of textiles. Digital imaging technologies are adding more layers to the process of print, weave, stitch and animation. We must keep aware of the expanding boundaries and be inclusive, rather than exclusive, allowing the boundaries to blur and sharpen and shift.

Title: Pink Silk
Size: 0.5 x 1.7 metres
Materials: wool felt and digital transfer print
Photo: David Ramkalawon

Title: Doll's coat
Size: 0.5 x 0.5 metres
Materials: wool felt
Photo: David Ramkalawon

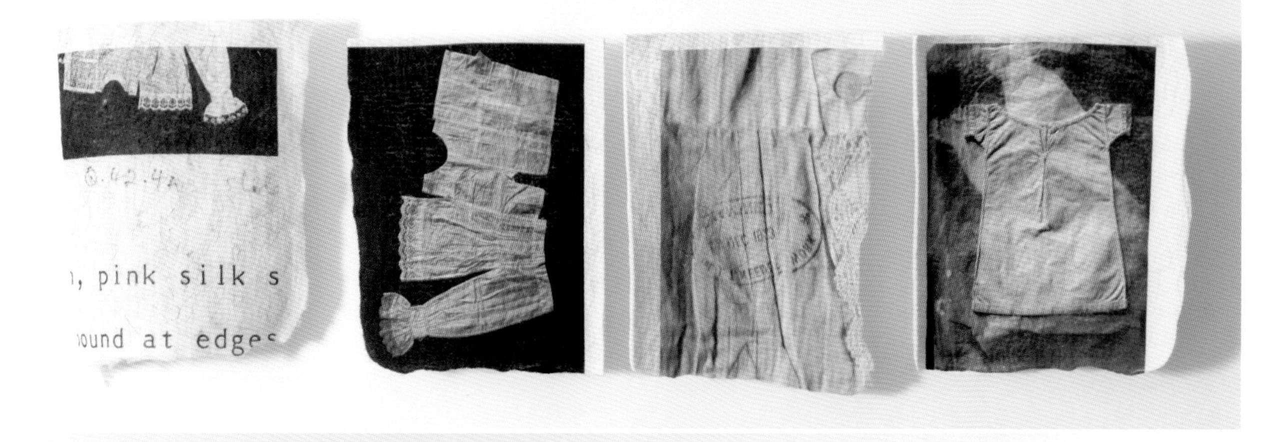
pink silk
at edges

Q) What is your most important personal memory of the making?
A) The way paint affects un-stretched canvas.

I come from a family of artists. Both parents worked during my childhood using a broad range of materials, textile was one of many. We had a home with a huge sitting room which was also our centre of creative activity. I remember there were both a hand loom and a large working table on which a hand sewing machine always sat. We children were encouraged to be a part of their work. My father became Vice Principal of Kingston College of Art and I grew up surrounded by his colleagues, students and the work of the college. To me this was a normal upbringing. We were all busy exploring our own creative interests. No particular material held precedence.

Title: Marsh Condition I – IV, 2011
Size: 1.15 x 1.1 metres
Materials: paint and stitch on canvas
Photo: Rod Bugg

POLLY BINNS.

On my degree course in Fine Art Sculpture I was preoccupied by rigid and flexible materials or the change which could occur through various processes. This was manifested in my degree show through clay and thread. During a post graduate diploma in Ceramics I also began to 'stitch' as a form of drawing and mark making. In my early professional years I attended an excellent adult education weaving class where woven structures began to take precedence and clay became a form of embellishment. A frustration with the process of weaving, the limitations of scale and the pace of working led to a shift into using artist's canvas. The scale of work grew and the extent to which I painted on the work. I had always used paint but it was at this stage that the painting process became integral to the development of the form and for me denotes the beginning of my mature work.

I have been a member of the 62 Group since 1980, and an Honorary Exhibiting Member since 2000. I feel the Group's history of activities and of membership reflect the shifts and changes which have occurred over the last 30 years to textile education, public arts funding opportunities, exhibition opportunities and interest in textile at international level.

My mum made our clothes and I was always aware of the feel of the fabrics and the smell. I loved to see her open up the dining table and lay out the patterns and start to cut. I can still hear and sense the sound of the scissors cutting through the paper and fabric and echoing on the table underneath. It seemed really special. I loved the sense of cloth against the skin, in both handling and wearing and was aware of this in the places and homes we visited. It was the beginning of a love of texture and surface I now realise, but it took many years to become the creative tool for me. There was never a real conscious decision to work in textiles really; my life flowed into the use of cloth as a means of expression after a conversation with a tutor on foundation course and I went on to take a degree in Embroidery. It is where I found myself and found myself as a person too I think.

HILARY BOWER.

I came to appreciate and love fabrics, the need to make my own 'fabric' or surface to then work/embellish. To sketch and 'think' through drawing and marking and the same applies within the use of cloth, stitch, along with other materials which I now employ. I realise that it is critical to my current work that there is a textile root and that it is visible to others, even in a simple, minimal way. It is also how that textile aspect has become connected to other materials which I hope is visible, seen and perhaps understood or that it encourages questioning in the mind of the viewer as to the relationship of the materials in front of them.

I became a member of the 62 Group in 1984. In that time the Group has maintained its fundamental belief in the use of stitch and cloth, but also has been open minded enough to shift and change with what has been happening in textile art over the years. This is what has kept it vital and helped it keep a secure and respected place in the world of art and textiles.

Title: In Silence (detail)
Size: 66 x 92 x 12 cm
Materials: linen, plywood, lead, aluminium
Photo: Dick Makin Imaging

Title: In Silence (right)
Size: 66 x 92 x 12 cm
Materials: linen, plywood, lead, aluminium
Photo: Dick Makin Imaging

My grandmother and her family were industrial weavers; they worked in a mill in Somerseat, Lancashire. As a child I visited the mill, witnessed at first hand the sight and smell of weaving. We also played a lot at home, with cloth and thread. My grandmother taught me to knit, sew and make things with cloth, often gifts for my mother. The importance of this early exposure is that I never considered Textiles as exclusively female. My grandmother's brother won several prizes for his weaving, he also had a small loom at home, that I can remember looking at and working with.

MICHAEL BRENNAND-WOOD.

It's also worth pointing out that all around our house were factories connected to the making of cloth, heavy engineering for the equipment used in the mills. My decision to work with cloth was also enhanced at Foundation, myself and another male student used to work ideas up in alternative media. The college had a weave department for the textile trade, we used to go in and ask how to make certain pieces. The tutor, I later found out had a connection with the Bauhaus. One of the pieces I made was a tapestry that I can remember being referred to as a Bauhaus Strip Tapestry.

I've always been interested in contested areas of textile practice: embroidery, pattern, lace and recently floral textiles. I've pioneered new ways of researching and developing ideas sourced from textile history. If you know your textiles you would recognise the fusion and allusion to textile culture in my work, drawn from all over the world. An awareness and respect certainly developed through travel. Many, many times I've been referred to as a maverick because people want to see the familiar. This is particularly true in textiles, a culture that seems to worship the remaking of existing artefacts. You can see so many references to historical textiles in my work, you might have to work at it but they are there in abundance.

I was invited to be an Honorary Exhibiting Member of the 62 Group around 1994 and enjoy its inclusivity, creativity and commitment to standards.

Title: A Flag of Convenience – The Sky is Crying, 2011
Size: 114 x 63 x 4 cm
Materials: embroidery, fabric, acrylic, toy soldiers, thread, resin on wood base
Photo: Peter Mennim

Title: Pretty Deadly, 2011 (right)
Size: 94 x 94 x 10 cm
Materials: embroidery, fabric, acrylic, toy soldiers, thread, resin, glass on wood base
Photo: Peter Mennim

I don't think I made a conscious decision to work within the discipline of textiles. Textiles and making was just part of growing up, and thinking about it, it makes a lot of sense why I do what I do. As well as my mum making clothes, her mum was a beautiful knitter, (would knit all the grandchildren school jumpers) and she also was a soft furnishing maker for a department store in Brighton. My dad's dad did upholstery for British Rail. There is an old armchair at my mums, Victorian I think, which is covered in British rail upholstery fabric, which my dads' dad recovered. Making, remaking, recovering and repair were done as a necessity as well as a pleasure.

LUCY BROWN.

At Goldsmiths College I discovered tapestry weaving and my own freehand weaving processes and developed language, which are still at the core of my practice. Weaving is employed as a language and method to reconstruct/ re-invent raw materials exploring ideas around re-telling/re-working histories, re-claiming/re-configuring female body image. Weaving by tradition is slow and labour intensive. I use time as part of my process. The time the work takes to make, is part of the end result. I use second hand and vintage clothing as raw material, to make tense, suspended woven 'offerings'. Sourcing, collecting, making are core motivations in the work. Raw materials are sourced from second-hand clothes shops, markets and fairs. These items are selected and deconstructed through actions of cutting, unpicking and ripping.

Free hand weaving is developed in response to my physical and emotional experiences with selected clothing. There is a seductive and obsessive drive with the raw materials, which fuels the desire to make and physically interact with the garments. From quite an early age I would dress up in my mum's, and her mum's wedding dresses. I still have both wedding dresses today.

The 62 Group, of which I have been a member since 2002, is very much about its membership taking ownership of the Group, and so is shaped by it current members. The Group has a freedom which allows it to be challenging, diverse, experimental.

Title: I lost myself because I wanted to be with you forever....
Size: 2.5 x 3.5 x 1 metres (variable by installation)
Materials: vintage and second hand garments including cotton velvet Laura Ashley dress and Marks & Spencer's 1970's negligées and lingerie · Rayon upholstery cord · glazing sprigs · steel tacks · dressmaking pins
Photo: David Ramkalawon

Title: I lost myself because I wanted to be with you forever....(detail as above)

Title: I lost myself because I wanted to be with you forever....(detail as above)

Supported by the Theo Moorman Trust for Weavers

My maternal and paternal grandmothers were skilled seamstresses and with large families and little money, most household textiles and clothes were home-made. Once there was more money and time, they both continued to sew recreationally and then focused on non-functional projects. I can't remember not being able to sew and make, everyone around me could sew, knit and crochet. We had very little money when I was small and my mum made all the popular toys of the day herself and all our dolls had nightdresses to match our own. For me, initially making my own clothes was my real interest, and I learnt to make and adapt clothes on my mum's Singer treadle as a pre-teen. Flares were out and drainpipes were in but there was no money to follow the whims of fashion in our house. I figured it out myself because although my mum was very skilled, I was incapable of letting her help me.

HAZELBRUCE.

This background and my textile training are very important to me, much more so now than 20 years ago. I have become much more proud of having a specialist textile training, specifically embroidery, than when I was younger. I sometimes felt the need to qualify or defend my choices, but not anymore. I feel part of an important community with a fascinating and multi-layered history and am immensely proud of that.

The starting point for my work is Material – found, bought, salvaged. At the moment I am looking at calico salvaged from print tables at my university because I am really interested in the unintentional and accidental mark, the life of cloth, what happens when cloth has multiple uses over its lifetime. This calico has layers of pattern and marks and none of them mine, which is important, I can respond to this large canvas of unintentional pattern making and accidental compositions.

I joined the 62 Group in 1991 and the Group has given me the opportunity and reason to sustain a practice when at certain points my life may have gone in a different direction. It has also been important to exhibit with peers, in selected exhibitions.

Title: From Collections (no 3) (below and detail)
Size: 148 x 150 cm
Materials: linen, cotton, silk · reclaimed
Photo: Dave Pauley – The Studio

As a child I taught myself to knit, sew and use a sewing machine, and in my teens I made most of my own clothes, using my grandmother's old Singer hand-operated machine (circa 1908!). However my family was not interested in anything creative and I went to an academic girls' school where art was considered unimportant. They convinced me I was no good at art and I studied, qualified and worked as a medical doctor. Consequently I only developed my interest in textiles rather late in life – in my mid 30's – and finally I did a degree in Textile Art in my mid 40's.

PENNY BURNFIELD.

Clothing and domestic textiles are so personal, literally the fabric of life. I have recently used my mother's sheets as a background onto which to project old family photographs. I hope to do something similar using worn tea towels. However, my textile origins are less important to me than they used to be. My work now utilises other media and I prefer to call myself an artist, working in textiles and mixed media. (I have recently used timber, paint, paper, found objects, and digital projection). But still, my roots are in textile art, it's what I know, where I turn to first when making something. It has also been a 'safe backdoor' into the world of art for me.

I joined the 62 Group in 2003 because it's the best! And I wanted to get to know and learn from other artists I respect. I think the members are continuing to push the boundaries with new approaches to textile art, more experimental media, and more challenging ideas. Sometimes we upset people. That's a good thing!

Title: Foxley 1 (above)
Size: 40 x 110 cm
Materials: withdrawn-threads and hand stitching on wool fabric
Photo: Tamara Bonnar

Title: Of Youth and Buried Time (above right)
Size: 100 x 50 cm (variable)
Materials: mixed media
Photo: Electric Egg

Title: Relative Density (right)
Size: 90 x 60 x 30 cm
Materials: mixed media
Photo: Michael Wicks

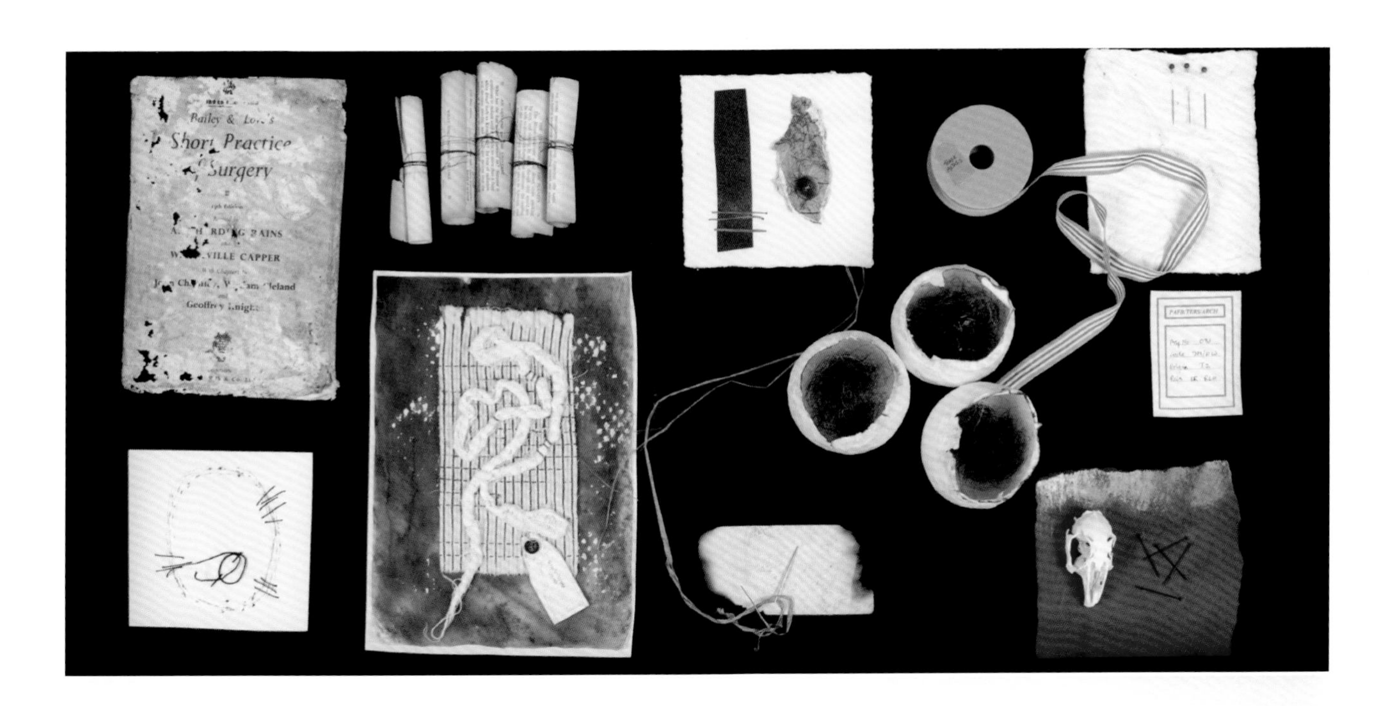
Bailey & Love's
Short Practice
Surgery

In my childhood in Bradford Yorkshire I had a friend whose grandparents lived in a classic 'back to back' cottage with stone flagged floors and an old leaded kitchen range. The interior of the cottage seemed very dark but a rag rug sitting on the flagged floor in front of the range looked like a jewel to me. In fact I suspect it was really quite subdued, but the colourful scraps of fabric intermingling with each other struck me as one of the most beautiful things I had seen. Many years later, short of money and in need of a new rug I remembered that rug and set about making my own. On completing the first one I couldn't wait to start the next and I soon realised that I had discovered a medium I loved. My mother, now in her nineties, made me promise that whenever I gave talks on my work I would be at pains to point out that it was in someone else's house that I had seen my first rag rug. For her generation they are associated with thrift and hard times rather than the ecologically sound style statement they have become.

JULIA BURROWES.

I studied painting and so was completely self-taught as far as textiles are concerned and had a wonderful time exploring the rich history and wide range of traditional techniques used in rag rug making. Although now I work less in rug making, I continue to use recycled materials. I actively dislike the throw away culture that results in such a terrible waste of resources. So many materials have a provenance which might be appreciated with a more reflective approach. Even the most humble of materials have had their moment and are part of a bigger history. I like to rescue and reinvent with them.

I joined the 62 Group in 1986 or 87 when I had just started to work in textiles. To join a group of reputable, informed, forward thinking people all engaged in textiles and organising their own exhibition was an absolute gift. Through the years we have worked to raise awareness of textiles as a medium worthy of serious consideration as a form of artistic expression.

Title: Sometimes (right and detail below)
Size: 50 x 65 cm
Materials: recycled paper
Photo: Michael Wicks

Title: nearly finished (detail, top left)
Size: 35 x 35 cm
Materials: Pina cloth, silk ribbon, silk floss
Photo: Dawn Robertson

Title: contemplation (detail, top right)
Size: 35 x 45 cm
Materials: Pina cloth, silk organza, sealing wax, linen and silk thread
Photo: Dawn Robertson

Title: ready to choose (detail, bottom, left)
Size: 45 x 45 cm
Materials: Pina cloth, silk organza, silk floss, linen thread
Photo: Dawn Robertson

Title: simply history (detail, bottom right)
Size: 50 x 50 cm
Materials: vintage ribbon, pina cloth, silk organza
Photo: Dawn Robertson

Cloth, stitch and making have been absorbed into my life and not manufactured. The role of making, stitching and breathing cloth came about because of my home background and subsequently my education. I could not wait for my siblings to be all at school so I would have my mom's undivided attention accompanied by the scrap box (she made nearly all our clothes both sewing and knitting), the button box, Singer sewing machine, my doll and cat. My aunt taught me to crochet at the age of four and I remember sitting on the window seat practising, with fine hooks and cotton perle on a reel. We also had races to see who could produce the longest piece of corking. My brother Rory always won primarily because he chose the thickest thread and I would always choose the finest... we had lots of thread around the house because my aunt had a great uncle Albert who worked in the mills and kept us well supplied.

AMANDA CLAYTON.

I can never remember my paternal grandmother without knitting in her hands and the same with Aunt Kate and her crocheting. My mother used to knit in the car, with me between her and dad in the front, and my brothers and sisters in the back... early 1960's before all the seatbelt rules. My whole child hood was about doing 'stuff'.

I am proud to have trained in the discipline of embroidery and am passionate about hand stitch; it is in context with my life, it is what has formalised my practice. Many people do not see how looking, selecting and drawing underpins all aspects of this practice. However, I do like the relationship of different practices to one another. There are generic references which inspire me: I love the strong contrast in lace and the use of positive/negative space. As I choose to work in white I find I use these elements to create contrast in my own work.

I have been a member of the 62 Group since 1990 and feel that we need to exhibit widely to get the message across that textile artists are alive and kicking.

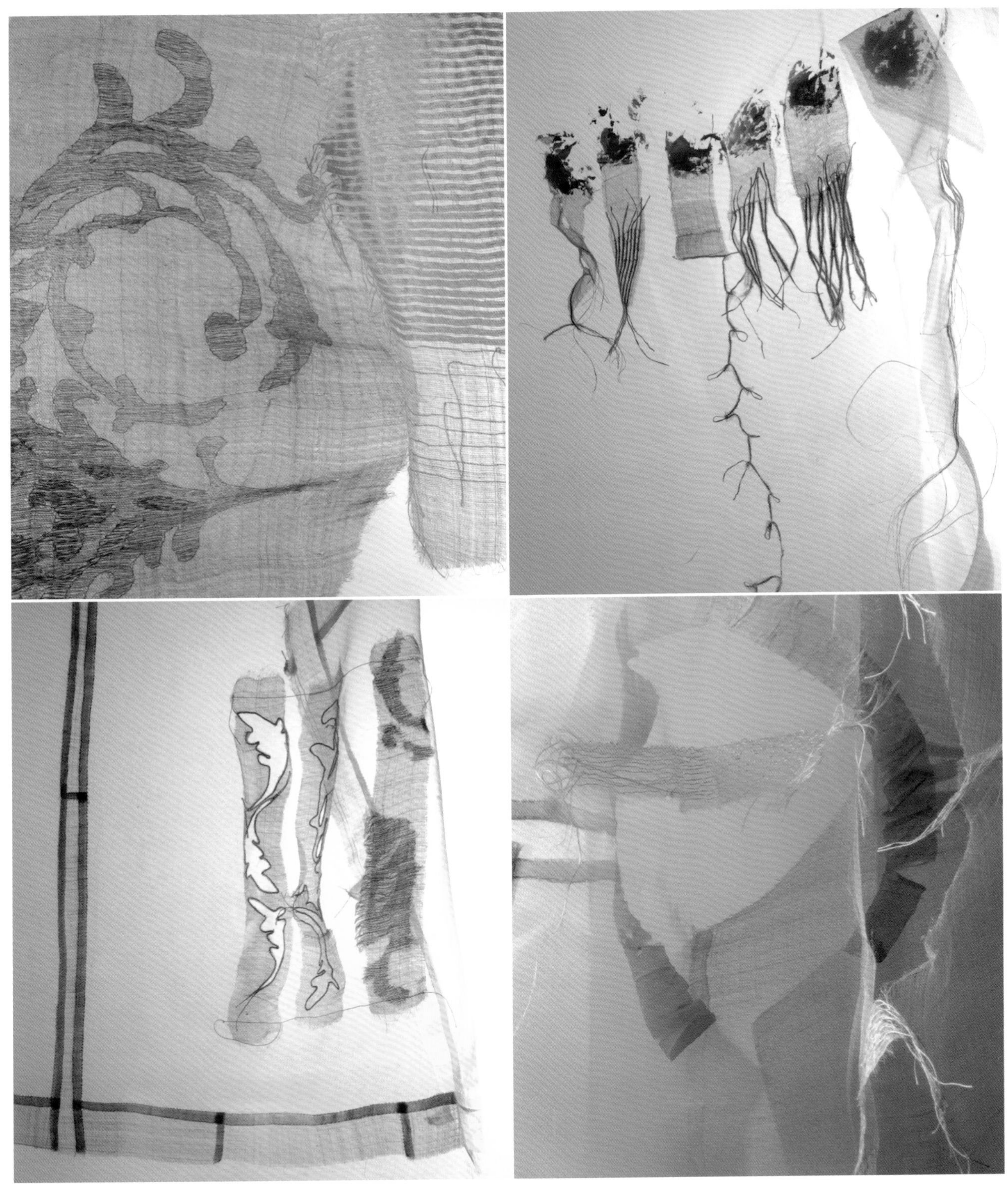

I originally studied 3D Design Ceramics at Farnham School of Art but eventually wanted to have more control over the results of my work and felt restricted working within a ceramic tradition. I was interested in using different materials and began to make handmade paper to create similar surfaces to my work in clay based on an organized equivalent of organic form. I started to combine the papers with collage, fabrics and then stitching.

Through a residency in the print room of the University of Central Lancashire I have become increasingly involved with using silk screen printing techniques. Although I have found Norma Starszakowna's exploration of the expressive qualities of print in her experimental mixed media pieces to be intriguing, I tend to look towards female fine artists who use materials and make objects for inspiration. The uncompromising textile pieces by Louise Bourgeois and her advice 'that pieces should liberate themselves from the decorative', and the ambiguity and unsettling nature of the unusual objects made by Cathy de Monchaux give me my references. However, for me the most influential textile artist is Rozanne Hawksley whose work is thought-provoking, innovative and mysterious.

Title: Faces
Size: 23 x 34 x 7 cm
Materials: fabric dolls faces, collage, and stitch
Photo: Peter Scott

Title: Stitched Faces Installation
Size: 150 x 120 cm
Materials: silk organza,silk,manmade fabrics,stitch and screen-print
Photo: Peter Scott

Title: Stitched Faces 2 (detail)
Size: 76 x 21 cm
Materials: silk organza,bandage and screen-print
Photo: Peter Scott

ELIZABETH COUZINS-SCOTT.

I applied to join the 62 Group in 1994 because of its reputation. Its selection process is rigorous but fair relying on different groups of members to make the selections at two stages. The criteria for membership, the exhibition programme and the selection process for each exhibition keeps me motivated to develop my work and ideas.

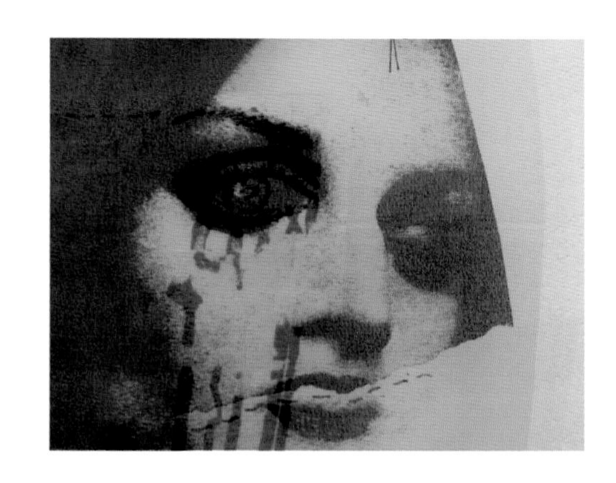

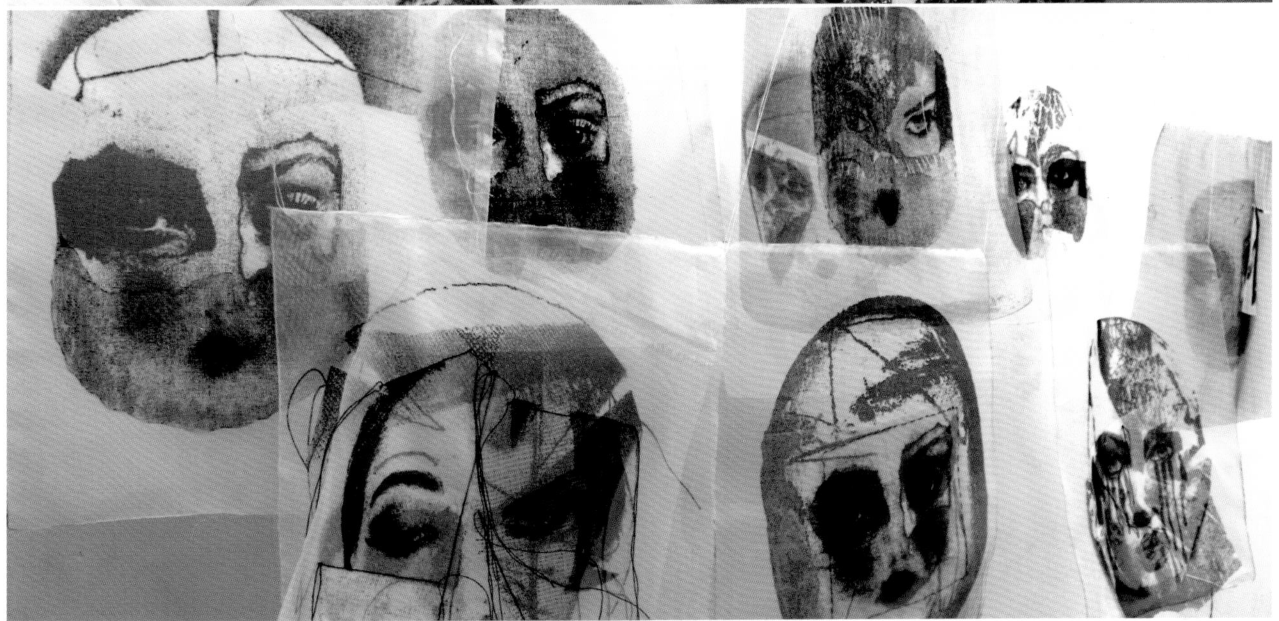

I grew up in a house where my mother was always making things: 'to be a good knitter you have to be a good ripper' was something I heard often. I remember her sending me out with a ball of cotton and a crochet hook after having shown me how to do the chain stitch. I worked a length of chain stitch and when I came back in (very proud of my work) my mother ripped it out and showed me how to do the next stitch. I was shocked, I learned other stitches and it taught me the lesson that I had to do it right from the start. When I have left work that I was not entirely satisfied with I have regretted not ripping it later.

DOROTHY ANNDALY.

I use Irish crochet techniques to make drawings, combining crochet with paper to make collages. My textile roots are very important to me, now that I live abroad. What you choose to make and how you make it can convey cultural identity. I love looking at old pieces of Irish crochet and thinking about the women who made the work and under what conditions they were working. Some of the very fine crochet that they produced is amazing. I love the way that whole families helped to make pieces and the fact that they were known by the motifs they specialized in. I find the history behind crocheting in Ireland really interesting. For me, it is the countless women who made crochet to sell, or sometimes for themselves that I find inspiring. In my own family the inspiration comes from my mother and aunts.

I joined the 62 Group in 1993 because I wanted to be in a group of people who were excited by the possibilities of textiles and to show my work with them. I hope the Group will continue to challenge the accepted ideas about what textile art is and present new and exciting work.

Title: Turn, 2011 (right)
Size: 4 x 4 x 10 cm plus strings
Materials: crochet cotton
Photo: Ulrike Sauer

Title: Petticoat, 2011 (below)
Size: 13.5 x 18.5 cm
Materials: crochet cotton, linen & embossed paper
Photo: Ulrike Sauer

I think I was born loving fabrics and stitch, and as no one in my family worked with cloth I sought out role models: a neighbour who was a dressmaker – by the time I was ten years old I made my own clothes and for my family. I loved it. Another neighbour gave me two 1940's embroidered dresses, and at fourteen I started collecting them, delighting in their detailing: pleats, gores, pin tucks, beautiful cloth and the hand stitching. A tailoress taught needlework at school, I was fascinated by the cutting of flat cloth shapes to construct jackets, and dresses, the subtle changes of sleeve shapes to create wonderfully different forms. These influences stay with me every day.

COLETTEDOBSON.

By using the language of cloth, ideas around textiles are discussed. My interests are in the construction of cloth, creating work that is formal and well made. Everything measured, marked, pinned, tacked, basted, stitched, pressed at every stage, tucked in seams, all matching patterns and textures, bound hems and buttonholes, unadorned, practical. An emotional attachment to particular fabrics – wool worsted, tweed, boucle, crepe, cotton poplin, flannelette and vest material, are constructed with sparse adornment. The work has its roots in textile history and practice, the language of cloth and stitch being the pivot, around which aspects of social history are expressed. The care and presentation of cloth in a domestic environment reflects social expectations, an outward expression of conformity to society's ideas. The viewer of the work would find recognisable and familiar objects put together to make them impossible to use, tea towels and soap, embedded with bristles and scrubbing brushes woven together. Utility being made impossible to use – a dichotomy of purpose. Expectations never to be achieved.

I joined the 62 Group in 2000 for the chance to join a debate that was offering new insights into textile practice. The Group provides opportunities for the public to see works that appreciate textiles and its heritage and an opportunity to debate issues of today in relation to the past.

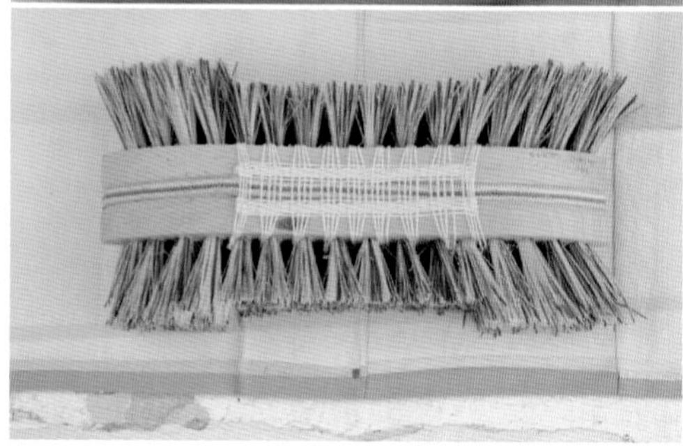

Title: And what is it you do? (detail, right)
Size: 40 x 7 cm
Materials: bristle and thread
Photo: Catherine Dineley

Title: And what is it you do? (detail, top)
Size: 10 x 30 cm
Materials: bristle
Photo: Catherine Dineley

Title: And what is it you do? (detail, above)
Size: 22 x 8 cm
Materials: thread and linen
Photo: Catherine Dineley

When I was very young my mother taught me to stitch, mend and embroider things for our home. Always making things from a young age meant, firstly, that holding a needle has always been natural and also that by the time I went to school I was quite good at sewing and therefore I never hated it like so many other young girls. But the deciding factor leading to a greater interest in textiles was my dismal failure in Latin in my rather traditional Girls' Grammar School, which meant I was 'demoted' to the B Stream and took Needlework at O Level.

My training in textiles, whilst art and design based, was nevertheless rooted in good technique and craftsmanship. I was taught/made aware of many traditional embroidery techniques and have always been inspired by those textile practices, both western and others, where the work demonstrates the makers' affinity with and understanding of the materials used, and where the creator's hand is evident, perhaps in slightly less-than-perfect results. I particularly respond to and learn from innovative and imaginative work made under constrained conditions, possibly when the materials available are limited.

I have never regretted the textile training I received, but I do find it hard sometimes to work as freely as I would like. I am particularly interested in the development of stitch, especially hand stitching, and see my work as part of the ongoing evolution since the mid 20th century, of stitched textiles as an expressive medium. Most of my work is based on my knowledge of different techniques that, in order to express my ideas and subject matter, I drastically alter and personalise - possibly to the point where the original technique is no longer recognisable. Thorough and ongoing research of my subject through drawing, photography and sampling is of paramount importance in my work.

JEANDRAPER.

I have been a member of the 62 Group since 1975 and have seen a movement towards less emphasis on stitch used alone but now excitingly combined with a greater range of different textile disciplines and mixed media. My hope is that the Group continues to grow and remains a strong reflection of contemporary textile practice.

Title: Tall Rock Forms
Size: 82 x 102 cm
Materials: dyed and painted cotton with machine and hand stitching
Photo: Mark Duffell

Title: Tall Rock Forms (detail, right)
Size: 82 x 102 cm
Materials: dyed and painted cotton with machine and hand stitching
Photo: Mark Duffell

I didn't have any particular textile influences as I was growing up, but I have since discovered my family dates back to the Huguenots and the silk trade.

I remember the first time I printed with a large scale open silk screen, saturating the fabric with dark blue dye paste. It was physically demanding and I felt absorbed in the process. The course at Goldsmiths gave a basic grounding in printing, weaving and embroidery, but the emphasis was on development of personal ideas and contextual studies. I experimented mainly with print processes and photographic silk screens using a De Verre camera.

I enjoy the directness and physicality of some of the more traditional processes I use, however I continue to develop new methods using a broad range of materials. I combine traditional dye pastes and pigments with more contemporary methods of image production and some heat press techniques. Although I am very connected to the textile processes that I experiment with, I do not feel defined by them. I am trying to communicate my thoughts, experiences and emotions and use the materials and processes that I find expressive.

DAWN DUPREE.

For several years I was making work that directly referenced the urban environment and included images of abandoned domestic objects, derelict buildings and wastelands. Layers of process abstracted and obscured any specific place, though suggested narrative and embedded imagery revealed a distinctly western experience. Interestingly, when I visited Lithuania for the Biennale a few years ago Great Britain, Brazil and South Africa were invited to exhibit alongside one another and the contrast was astonishing. For example, several artists from Brazil had been very resourceful and recycled found materials where others were not available, to produce exquisite textile artworks.

I joined the 62 Group in 2003 in order to exhibit alongside and feel connected to other textile artists, and to engage people in the conversation and diversity of contemporary textile art.

Title: Maternal (top)
Size: 117 x 77 x 4 cm
Materials: dye paste, pigments, flocking, printed on linen
Photo: Dawn Dupree

Title: Turbulence (above)
Size: 119 x 77 x 4 cm
Materials: dye paste, pigments, flocking, printed on linen
Photo: Dawn Dupree

Title: Domestic Bliss (right)
Size: 105 x 76 x 6 cm
Materials: dye paste, pigments, flocking, printed on furnishing satin
Photo: Dawn Dupree

Over the last two decades I have increasingly felt that working in textiles was something I had to do, as though innately within me. Looking at my upbringing and my family, it would be obvious to an outsider why this should be so.

I remember, from an early age, my mother sewing, making and knitting, and was always intrigued when she sat watching the television whilst not actually looking at her knitting needles! Of course, she made most of her daughters' dresses from childhood up to their weddings. When we were young she was a home worker, with an industrial sewing machine in her bedroom. At the end of the day when my twin sister and I had walked home from junior school, we had to pick up all of the loose threads from the carpet; we both hated that job! My mother's sister was a very talented needlewoman and my three sisters are also very capable with the needle.

CARENGARFEN.

Going back a further generation, my maternal grandmother suddenly began to create textile collages in her seventies; she even incorporated her own hair in them. She became something of a celebrity in the area where she lived, and had a story written about her work in the local press as well as a large exhibition at the Whitechapel Library. The exhibition was successful and she sold a good deal of artwork.

Over the last couple of years I have become more and more aware of my traditional roots. I feel that making, sewing and creativity have been embedded in my psyche by my ancestors; and this allows me to cut material without fear, to make seams, to hem and to create paper patterns even when I have no formal training or practice in these. These roots are of vital importance to me now. I use traditional crafts, sewing and printing, and transform them into contemporary artworks.

I joined the 62 Group in 2008 and consider that it is going from strength to strength in its quest to maintain the quality of work of all exhibiting members.

Title: Main Course, Wafer Thin, A Study of the Role of Fat, (unravelled), 2012 (right)
Size: 10 x 0.31 metres
Materials: cotton, SF20 binder, pigments, silk threads
Photo: Ahlburg Photography

Title: Main Course, Wafer Thin, A Study of the Role of Fat, (open), 2012 (detail top)
Size: 10 x 0.31 metres
Materials: cotton, SF20 binder, pigments, silk threads
Photo: Ahlburg Photography

Title: Real Life 1, 2012 (below)
Size: 25 x 28 cm
Materials: cotton, SF20 binder, pigments, silk threads
Photo: Ahlburg Photography

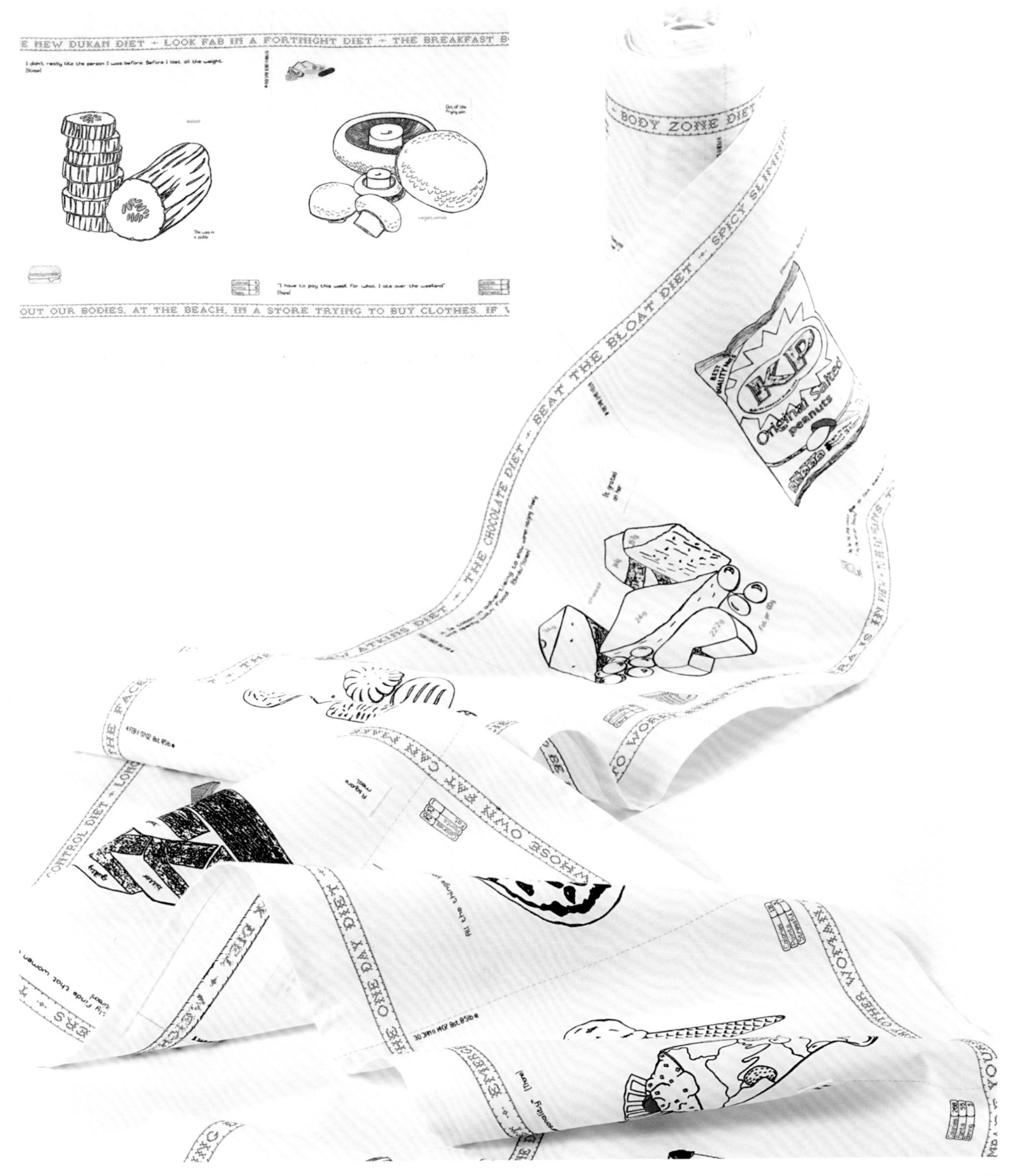
E NEW DUKAN DIET ✣ LOOK FAB IN A FORTNIGHT DIET ✣ THE BREAKFAST
OUT OUR BODIES, AT THE BEACH, IN A STORE TRYING TO BUY CLOTHES. IF
"I have to pay this week for what I ate over the weekend"
BODY ZONE DIET
ATKINS DIET ✣ THE CHOCOLATE DIET ✣ BEAT THE BLOAT DIET ✣ SPICY SLIMMING
KP Original Salted peanuts
WHOSE OWN FAT CAN MAKE
CONTROL DIET

As a child I was always making things – clothes, pictures, little fabric characters – and my mum was always making things too. She was keen to teach me all her sewing skills, so encouraged me to take other subjects at school. Sewing was something I did in my spare time. My granny used to save her pressed powder boxes and I would carefully cover these in Liberty print remnants. For my sixth birthday my parents bought me an old Singer sewing machine · the same year they bought my brother a skateboard. Now I have kids of my own, six seems incredibly young, but I guess my parents could see I just loved making things and they encouraged me because they are also very creative. I had complete confidence in my own ability, but for what ever reason I didn't see textiles as a career path.

EMILY JO GIBBS.

I started making fashion accessories in textiles and metal in the final term of my degree. On graduating I felt my skills didn't easily transfer to a job, so I briefly studied shoe making and leatherwork in Leicester and Walsall. However my degree show had received a very positive response so in 1993 I moved back to London and embarked on setting up my own handbag making business with the help of a Prince's Trust Loan. That was the beginning of a hectic decade, a vast amount of making hours, very steep learning curves with hugely exciting and glamorous moments.

I applied to join the 62 Group in 2006 because I was at a turning point. I had stopped making handbags and had just created a whole new body of work, which was for a new audience; I found it quite traumatic not defining myself as a handbag maker anymore. I wasn't quite sure how to define myself and wondered if a group of textile artists would have me! I felt I needed to be part of a critical peer group; I am really delighted I was selected to be a member, being part of the group challenged me to make new work at quite a difficult time.

Title: Billy (right)
Size: 25 x 30 cm
Materials: cotton sheet, silk organza, fabric paint, cotton thread
Photo: Michael Wicks

Title: Fred (below)
Size: 22 x 30 cm
Materials: cotton sheet, silk organza, fabric paint, cotton thread

Title: Woodland Group
Sizes & Materials: Silver and Willow Basket 12.5 x 20 cm
Sterling Silver and Willow Reed Warbler 11 x 22 x 90 cm
Sterling Silver and Silk Song Thrush 26 x 10 x 15 cm
Photo: Heini Schneebeli

Life isn't fair don't let that make you mad
be generous
be sensitive to others
show your empathy
you are a winner
don't be defeatist
be patient
be magnanimous
be in control of your feelings, be calm
Believe in yourself
you have great talent
practice work hard
don't rush it takes time to
keep playing be sporting
your looks will fade, but friends endure. be loyal
you don't need things to be happy
you love music be free sing, run, climb
Love and embrace life
be a good friend
be honest and honourable
Things don't always go to plan
you can be what ever you want - just work hard - be tenacious
ejg 2011

My mother and paternal grandmother were both skilled embroiderers, dressmakers and knitters who used transfers and patterns as the basis of their work. Personally, I found these methods too restricting and uncreative, and this, combined with uninspiring needlework lessons at school, almost put me off textiles altogether. I originally studied ceramics, and then, during the 1970's, was given a book on quilting. It showed ways of raising the surface, creating texture and incorporating non-textile elements into the work. This opened my eyes to the exciting possibilities of using cloth creatively of which I'd previously been unaware. I went back to study and was lucky to have inspirational tutors, for example Carole Whitehill, Maisie Hulmston and Maxine Bristow who encouraged experimentation, innovation and pushing the boundaries. I became aware of the marginal role of textile practice within contemporary art and began to exploit this position in order to subvert preconceptions of textile practice.

ANN GODDARD.

Although the history of textile practice informs the content of my work, I am also interested in the connection of materials and processes to wider issues. This has led to work which the viewer may not necessarily recognise as having textile roots. Much of my work has evolved from questioning the role and function of boundaries – boundaries in the landscape, boundaries between art and craft, boundaries between genres and historical boundaries between men and women's work. The content, materials and techniques, for example stitch and other textile elements such as felted silk paper, are used to reference textile practice in general rather than embroidery specifically and are employed strategically as carriers of ideas.

Since I joined the 62 Group in 2005, the Group has begun questioning the relevance of calling ourselves 'textile' artists. Because of my border position I have never really known what to describe myself as, but I know I personally need the parameters of textile practice as an underlying influence on my work. I hope the 62 Group continues to promote, and encourage awareness of, contemporary art practice using or referencing textile elements and processes in the broadest sense.

Title: Consequences (details, below and right)
Size: variable. Installation comprising 300 different sized units
Materials: felted cotton fibres, bristles, concrete
Photos: Ann Goddard

Title: Sun Dance (top and detail)
Size: 1 x 1.75 metres
Materials: hand dyed cotton, threads
Photo: Dominic Harris

Title: Green Circled (bottom and detail far right)
Size: 1 x 1 metres
Materials: hand dyed cotton, threads
Photo: Colin Harvey

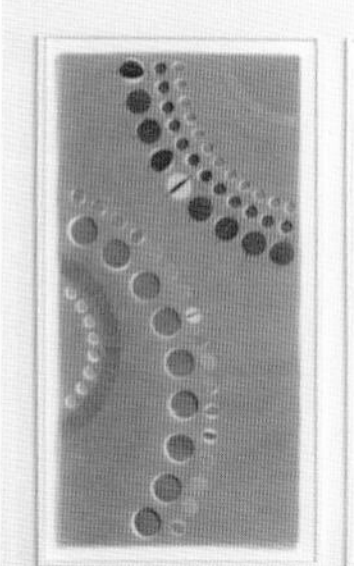
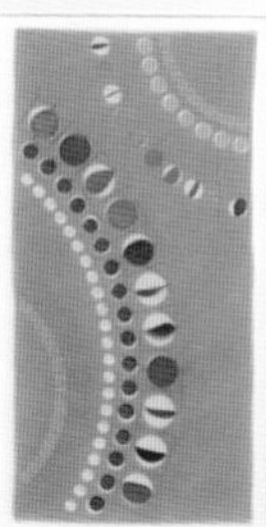
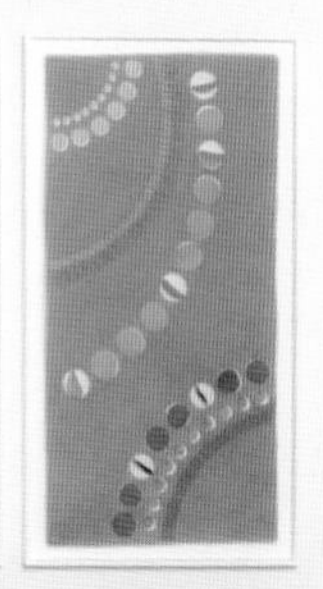

Sewing has always been present in my life, along with the satisfaction of making and creating. My mum had a sewing room when we were little, a tiny narrow room, with shelves seemingly scaling the high walls, box upon box of fabric with space near a small window for a table and machine. I remember she sewed a beautiful name on my standard issue, dull, drab comprehensive grey PE skirt, a task required by the school. She stitched it in red chain stitch on the dark grey fabric, it was beautiful, the most lovely in the class. I never thought of my mother embroidering before that. When I first learnt to use the sewing machine instead of making anything practical I drew triangles in pink and grey zig-zag, an important personal memory to me.

RACHELGORNALL.

I recently learnt that my maternal great grandmother trained as a seamstress and was given her Jones hand sewing machine. A beautiful piece of machinery, with so many important connections and history, a treasured possession and one which I hope will be involved in making my work at some point in the future.

I think the ever-present joy of making, and an enjoyment of textiles on a practical level, has been passed down to me. This has definitely influenced my use of textile as a creative medium.

The use of craft skills and a connection with the process of making, with the creation of the work itself, is very important to me and to the work. The enjoyment of creating 'things', the ability to control colour through the dyeing process and to experiment with colour, line and form through dyeing, cutting and stitching are all very important. I utilise the properties of translucent fabrics, together with the mark of hand cut patterns and hand stitch to explore and celebrate pattern and shape. The mark of the 'maker', and a respect for the material and process is vital to the work that I make and to my creative being.

I joined the 62 Group in 2008 in order to experience the rigour of exhibiting as part of a group promoting excellence and alongside artists of such high calibre.

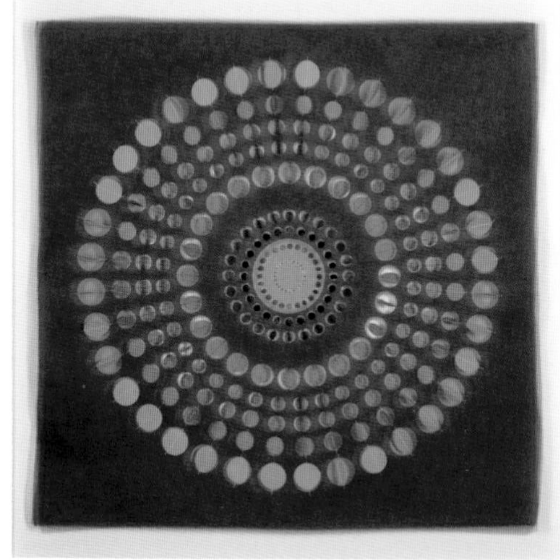

I trained in weave at Goldsmiths College as a mature student and my current work references that training. These textile roots are extremely important for me and I hope that the viewer would be aware of this when looking at my work. A female weaving in a fine art context speaks volumes before any work is placed on the wall. I find textiles are loaded with cultural identity, which is why I find work in this area so interesting and challenging; textiles that reference strong social and cultural links are those that inspire me. Philosophy and psychoanalysis provide starting points for my work, which I contextualise through the work of other artists. Those that have been most influential for me have been Louise Bourgeois, Agnes Martin, Yinka Shonibare and Magdalena Abakanowicz. Barnett Newman and the Abstract Expressionists explored their own inner journeys through their free flowing gestures. These contrast with the regular gesture of the weave and the two together create their own aesthetic.

CHRISTINE GORNOWICZ.

I joined the 62 Group in 2009 as I felt it provided a forum for more developmental work and I hope in the future there will continue to be a place within the Group for conceptual approaches to textile art.

Title: Miasma- the mark of existance (right)
Size: 44 x 40 cm
Materials: linen and monofilament ikat weave
Photo: Ben Edwards

Title: Sunteino- the tension of the unknown (below)
Size: 69 x 45 cm
Materials: linen and monofilament ikat weave
Photo: Ben Edwards

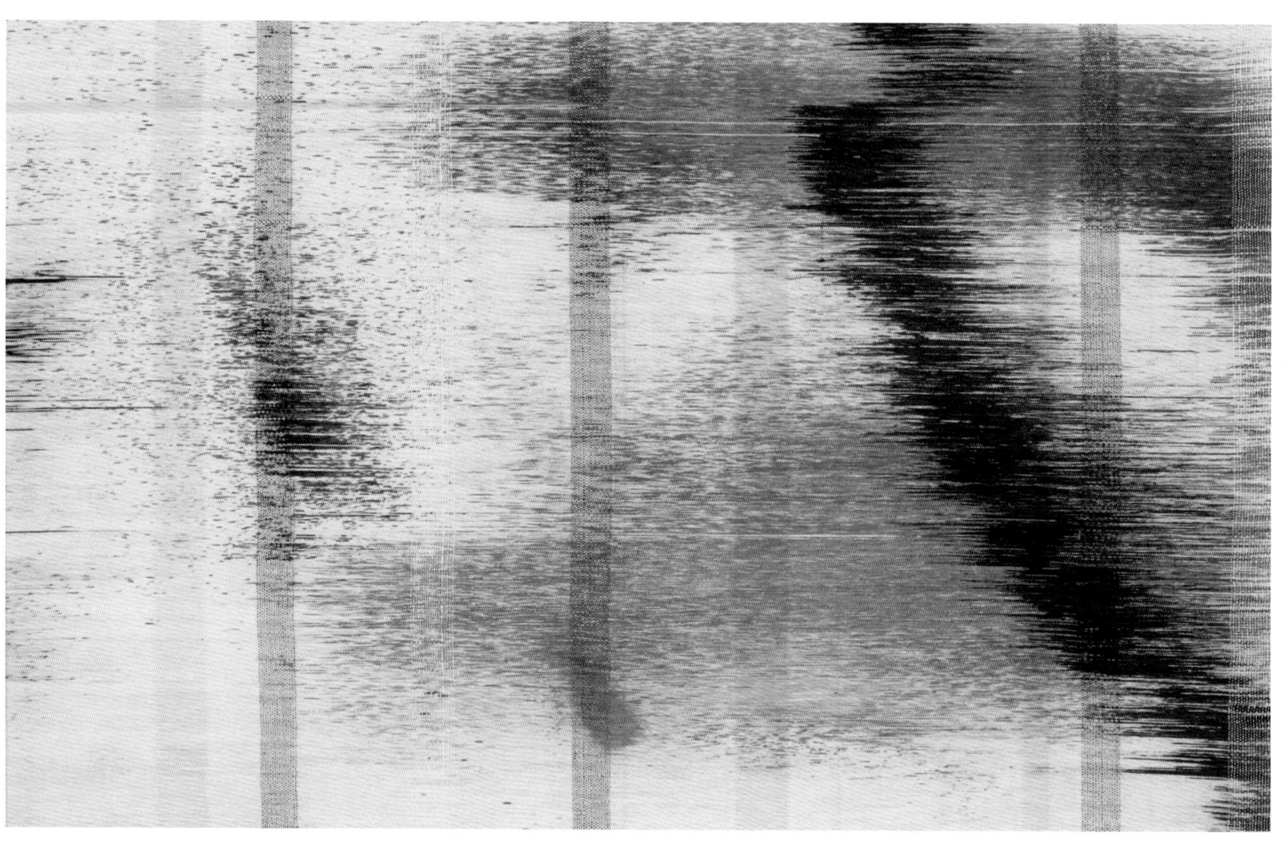

My much loved grandma – Alice Hunter – sewed by hand and treadle machine the oblongs of fabric that magically turned into sailor's collars. These were of blue denim with a striped cotton reverse, plus a number of loops and lengths of tape for fixing as well as the three surface white stripes out-lining the top collar (these were often said to represent Nelson's main victories) which had to be slip-stitched onto the fabric. My mother and Aunt Winnie constantly sewed and knitted – clothes and household 'linen', and embroidered – usually with Anchor Floss using an iron-on decorative transfer that left an image made up of blue dots – usually a favourite 'crinoline lady', a thatched cottage, a dog or a bowl of flowers.

ROZANNE HAWKSLEY.

I obtained a Degree in Fashion from the Royal College of Art but I hated the 'fashion scene' and the 'fashion business'. Years later I joined a three-week summer school which was led by David Green at Goldsmiths College. I was over 40 and this changed my life. I started with somewhat wild prints springing up from or dredged up with difficulty from my mind. He gave me a key to a door beyond which lay... WHAT!

'Textile practices' influence my way of working. My response and emotional awareness can start my visualisation; then looking for THE thing: the materials, colour, mood, the instinctive inexplicable feeling that YES – this is it – this is right.

I joined the 62 Group in the late 1970's but resigned after a few years, feeling that my work was out of line with the rest of the Group. Now all methods, materials are accepted if the work is seriously and honestly committed. Barriers have been broken down in the use of stitch and fabric, leading to overall inclusion of artists/craftsmen normally seen as painters, sculptors, ceramicists. In 2003 I was invited to rejoin as an Honorary Exhibiting Member.

So, how do we view the Group's direction? Will the need to encourage new directions and ways of working dissipate? Or lead to an absolute use of pure traditional stitch – a resurgence ? Good luck and clear thinking to us all.

Title: He always wanted to be a soldier
Size: Two parts, both 21 x 21 cm
Materials: mixed media
Photo: Michael Wicks

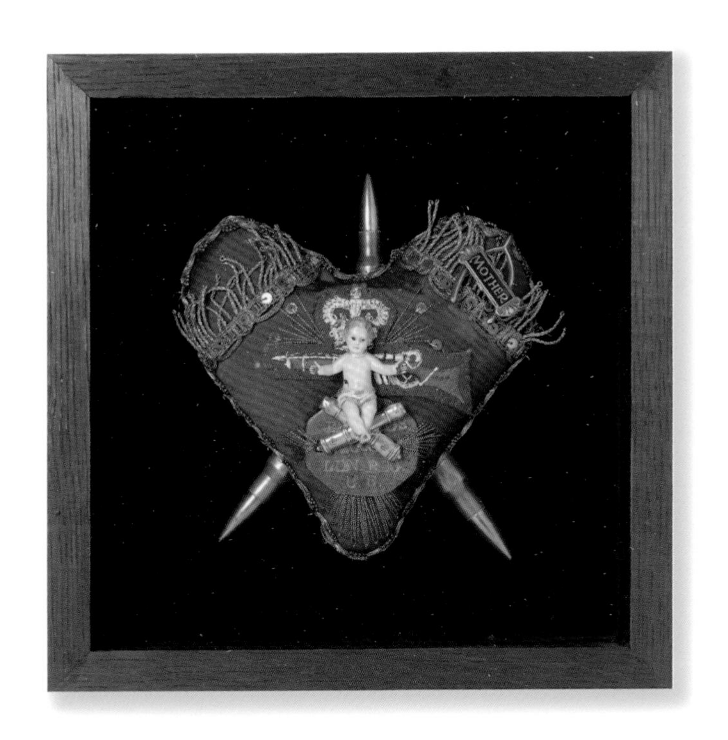
MOTHER

My original training was in textiles, with an initial focus on its three-dimensional structures. This work intersected with my interest in architecture. Around the same time I began to think more closely about the context and space of the work, and also to make site specific works. Together these interests lead to my current practice and prompted my returning to university in order to have the time to develop this thinking. In 2004 I completed an MA in Architecture and Spatial Culture.

MAGGIEHENTON.

My current practice involves enquiries into the particularities of place identity and with the ways in which place is constructed and inhabited. It is in part an enquiry into the material culture of a specific site, with an especial interest in architecture, domestic space and modes of inhabitation. Work has increasingly focused on residencies and on contexts in which I have been invited to make a response to site. Working methods have included: drawing, digital photography, print, stitch, mixed media constructions and installation. I often find myself working at the edge of my technical knowledge and with unfamiliar materials and techniques. However, there is a sensibility and an aesthetic which is informed by my earlier textile training.

Material culture forms the substance and the markers of place and identity. And, whilst the 'decorative and domestic' is the despised other of a modernist agenda, we have all read our post-colonial theory and understand the central (but denied) role of 'the other' in maintaining economic and cultural life. Textiles have a central role in forming the elemental structures of culture: shelter (clothing and housing), food production and transportation. The domestic is the ground upon which economic and cultural life depends.

I joined the 62 Group in 1987 in order to work with like-minded people. During my membership I have made many strong friendships and my time on the committee and other work for the Group has developed many valuable skills. The strength of the Group, and the reason that we have lasted 50 years, is its capacity to evolve and to remain vibrant and responsive to the shifts in art practices.

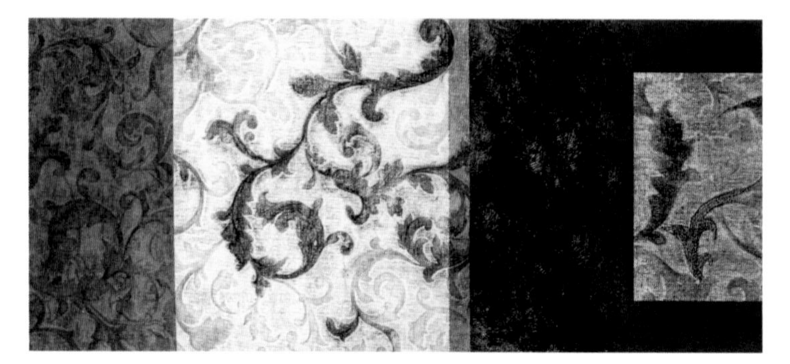

Title: Home-Land, May 2008 – Bundanon Trust, Australia (right)
Size & materials: detail from installation, leaves, bark, pins, chair
Photo: Maggie Henton

Title: Patterns of Inhabitation - London House, 2010 (left)
Size: 30 x 62 cm
Materials: From a sequence of print/collages using details taken from the walls of an Edwardian London house
Photo: Maggie Henton

My mother was always sewing when I was a child. She made lots of our clothes as well as making curtains and re-upholstering furniture. I was quite often by her side watching and helping. I enjoyed needlework at school and remember feeling a great sense of achievement when I managed to make some of my own clothes. I still have memories of those items and the fabrics that I used. I remember appliquéing a desert island image onto the back of a kimono I had made at school, orange and black satin on blue. I thought it looked great.

MICHELLE HOUSE.

I studied Textiles at Goldsmiths College, where I was able to try out many disciplines such as embroidery, felt-making and weave, but it was print that drew me in and inspired me. I felt that I had at last found the medium in which I wanted to express myself. I enjoy the hands on process of printing and I'm glad that I have the practical skills, especially since so much is digitally produced these days and I have continued to print since leaving college. I sometimes think that I might start printing onto paper as it is much less labour intensive than textile printing, but I find it far less inspiring, so textiles will probably always feature in my work.

I joined the 62 Group in 1999 and hope it will continue to promote textile artists work and to find further venues in which to show - not necessarily galleries - maybe empty shops, corporate spaces, hospitals or who knows one day our own space.

Title: Yellow Diagonal
Size: 1.2 x 2.9 metres
Materials: dyes and pigments printed and painted on to linen, drill cotton satin, barkweave cotton and wool flannel.
Photo: FXP

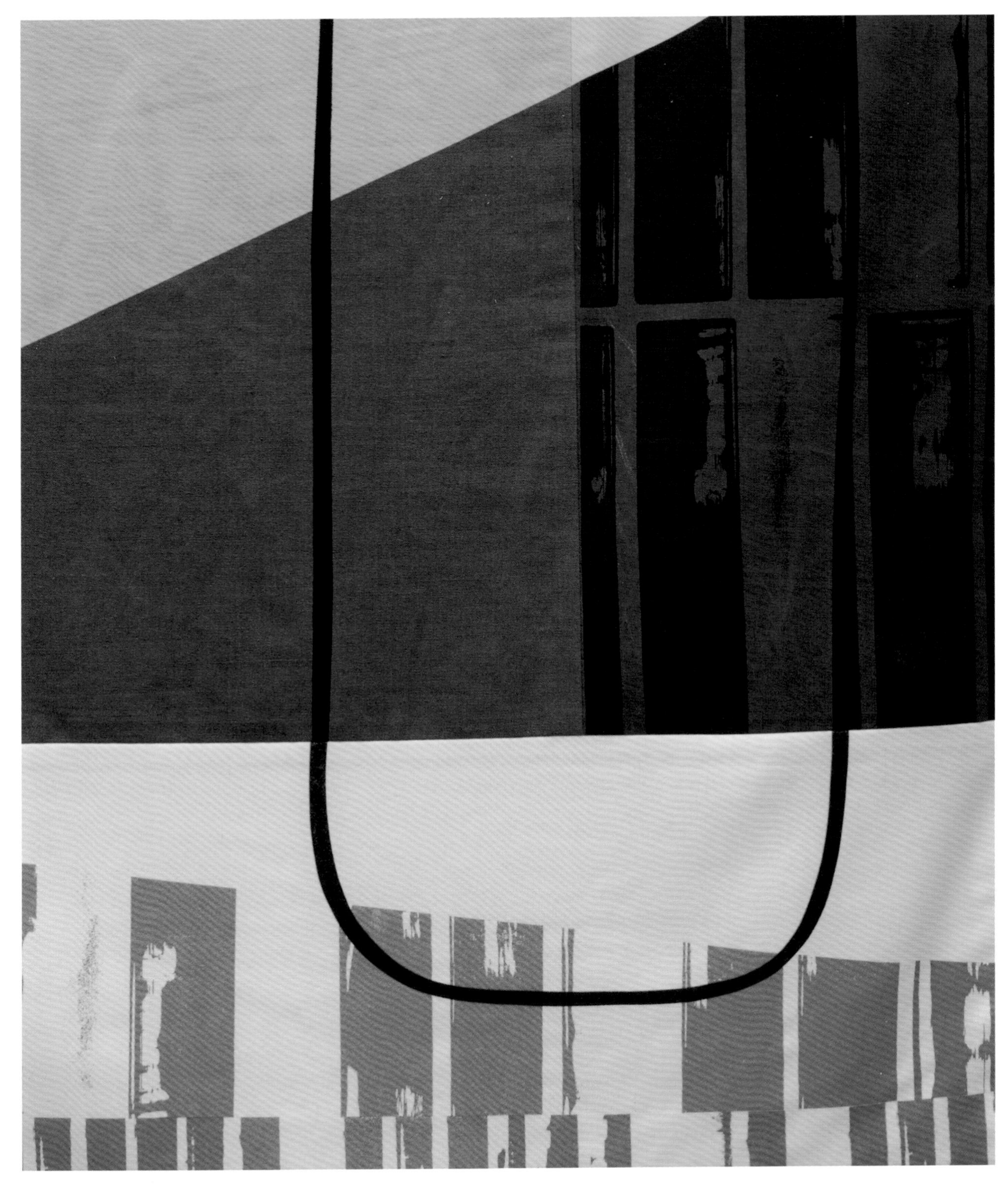

I was about 9 years old when I first started using my mum's old Singer sewing machine; I made a ragdoll and outfits for her. I loved choosing the patterned fabrics and designing the clothes. I felt excited to sit at the machine and turn the handle with one hand and feed the fabric with the other and make an idea. It was frustrating though, as my dressmaking skills were limited! I was always trying to make new (but rubbish) inventions like my high heeled socks, where I stitched a cotton reel on to the heels of my socks and walked round the garden tripping up and getting soggy feet!

RACHAEL HOWARD.

I have always loved sketching and colouring in. I started with the usual felt tips or crayons and then paper collage, creating patterns and textures, and then using actual fabric and becoming totally immersed in the variety of patterns and textures available. From an early age I was combining my sketches with fabrics, and throughout my years at college I was always experimenting with ways to join the two together in a satisfactory way. It wasn't until I left the RCA in 1992, and travelled to India, then returned and made a series of wall-hangings, that I developed the technique that I still use. I really wanted to capture the energy of a sketch and transfer that into textiles, and I felt I'd finally found a way!

My work has always been about things that are going on around me - personal or outside events happening in life, so subject matter is of our time. I execute my work in quite a low tech way, using pencil and paper, hand screen-printing and manual sewing machine, I like this way of working, but I am now also exploring digital imaging and computerised production which is exciting.

I joined the 62 Group in 1995 in order to continue the opportunity of exhibiting my work and to get it seen by a wider audience. I was chuffed to be selected and still am!

Title: Captain Brocolli (above)
Size: 21 x 31 cm
Materials: hand screen-printed sketches, various appliquéd fabrics and machine embroidery
Photo: R. Howard

Title: Catbrella (right)
Size: 21 x 31 cm
Materials: hand screen-printed sketches, various appliquéd fabrics and machine embroidery
Photo: R. Howard

I studied sculpture, and regard myself as a sculptor as much as a textile artist. Textiles have, however, always been dominant in my work. Cloth is enormously evocative, and as one of our very first experiences in life, it is familiar, comforting, and seductive. Incorporating textiles into my sculpture encourages public engagement with work that explores complex and difficult ideas. I am very interested in the concept of sewing and embroidery as gender based, and in re-appropriating cloth and 'female' techniques to make political comment. I use textiles in conjunction with other sculptural materials, employing processes that are traditionally a male preserve. Materials include timber, plaster, resin, copper, and forged steel, used in combination with textiles to create a visual paradox.

AL JOHNSON.

My sculpture is a response to contemporary and historical issues, and I am particularly interested in the collective memory, and how the past remains embedded in the present. I work in thematic series, and central considerations are the emotional outcome of war and the influence of religious doctrine.

I learnt to sew and embroider as a child. My mum was a great needle-woman, she could embroider, make clothes, toys, and make repairs. She never threw any cloth away, however small the scraps, and the rag-bag was a great delight. After my parents died I found the bag of felt scraps (felt, being expensive, was a prized commodity) that I used with my mum, and it is possibly the most evocative item that I kept; it has the smell of my childhood. We kept even the tiniest pieces of felt for toy's eyes, or decorations, and whilst this was due to financial privations to some extent, it was more importantly about the great value placed on materials and making.

I joined the 62 Group in 2008 and it is great that the Group has stood the test of time. It was radical from its outset and those radical beginnings are restated through our critical support for each other.

Title: Downed
Size: 4.25 x 3.65 x 3 metres
Materials: knitted textiles, stitched textiles, timber, forged steel
Photo: Aliki Braine

My mother was always making clothes or items from the many materials. She collected threads, buttons and other interesting goodies which she would let me use. I can remember making small textile pieces with her and the enjoyment of seeing the images grow from using threads, the act of creating and achieving.

CLAIRE JOHNSON.

I trained in embroidery but also this included experiencing other textile disciplines. I had at that time a special interest in quilting and soft sculpture, but we had to gain a full understanding of most textile techniques including its cultural history and the ability to use it in a creative but highly skilled manner. My work usually relates to exploring techniques but using a more contemporary twist, I enjoy making the materials to use and creating embellishments.

I love the Elizabethan methods, images, amazing skills and beautiful textile pieces; also I continue to marvel at the samples the very young produced. These still continue to intrigue me today. However I am also inspired by new technologies and the multitude of ways others use materials in a fine art manner there being no boundaries between the different art disciplines. I try to include an element of fun and if possible something that will draw the viewer in to the work or allow them to alter it/ participate. My work is really a continuing life journey of my experiences and interests.

I joined the 62 Group in 1981 and have watched as the Group has continued to promote the contemporary development of fine art textiles in the 21st Century but ensuring that the technical skill and individual ideas are of the highest level to promote excellence but to encompass both the fine art and textile discipline – there being no barriers. It is good to see a range of ages and acceptance of other's ideas, but also enjoyment of how a young artist gaining their feet within the Group and art world, achieves success to be able to move off to expand their work as a solo artist.

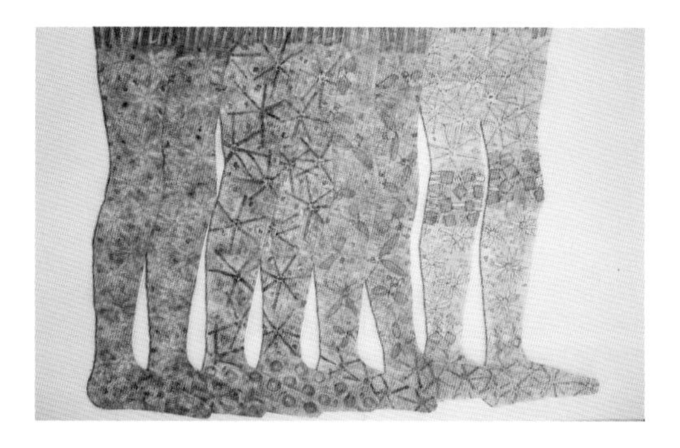

Title: Taking line for a walk · 4 pairs of stockings, 2010 (above and detail, right)
Size: Each 100 x 20 cm
Materials: transfer adhesive, paper, silk, machine stitching
Photo: Claire Johnson

Title: Money's Gloves, 2011 (above right)
Size: 35 x 12 cm
Materials: silk, transfer adhesive, dissolvable fabric, machine stitching and paper
Photo: Claire Johnson

Title: Oldham Gloves, 2011 (above left)
Size: 35 x 12 cm
Materials: maps, transfer adhesive, silk felt, dissolvable fabric and machine stitching
Photo: Claire Johnson

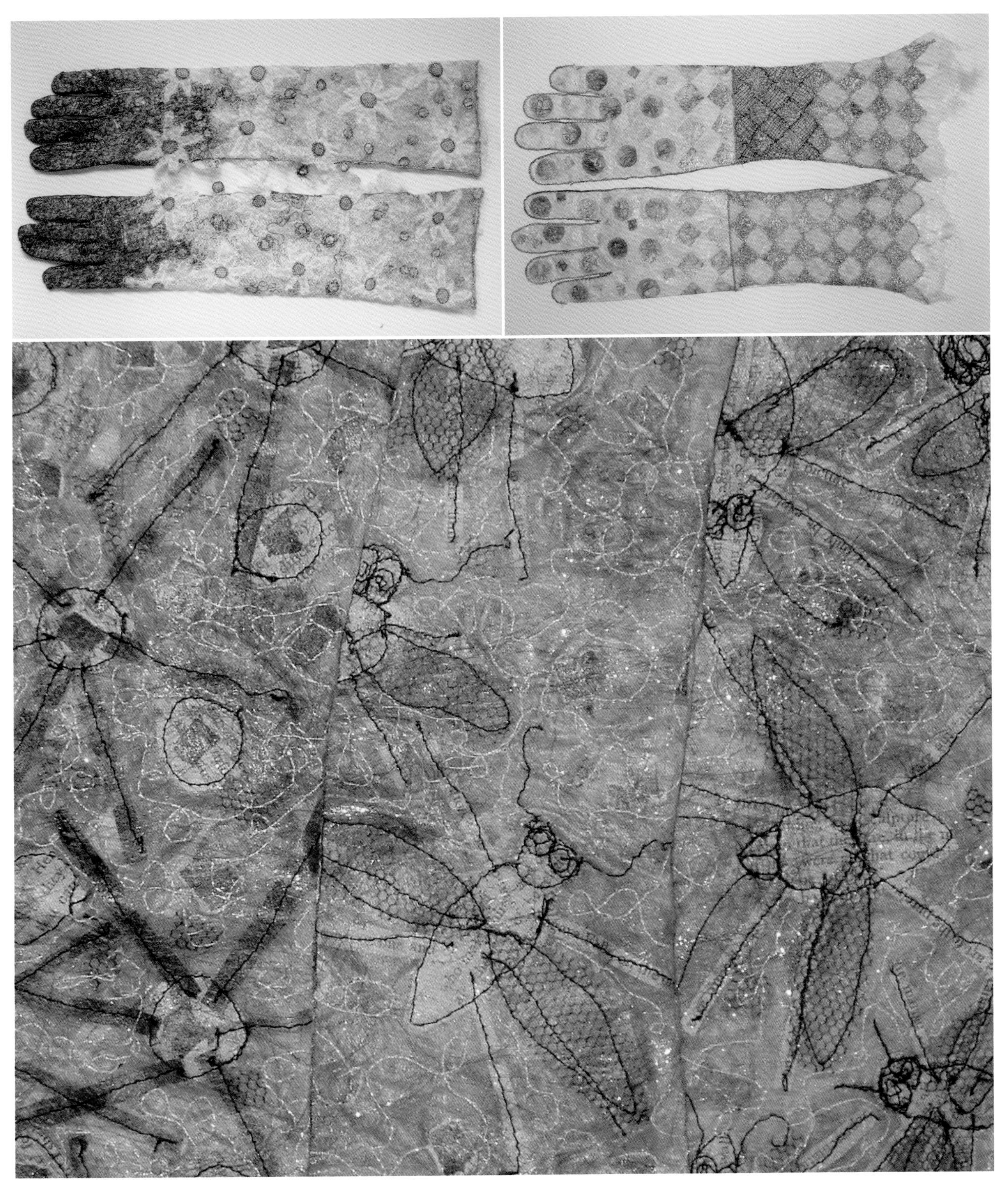

My mother loved making, she used to jump on the train and go to Liberty's in London and buy remnants and samples. She made my sisters and I matching Liberty print dresses and we made puppets, pictures, collages and animals with the offcuts. We always had to be doing useful things, always making. I realise that these influences were formative and not entirely uncritical since we had to visit galleries constantly to appreciate the current, the unconventional and the history of good art (indeed we queued overnight to see the Treasures of Tutankamen). She saw the connection of art to life without separation, she saw that by exposing young people to good design and art they could make informed choices in associated areas of life, in their relationships and decision making. She saw the importance of culture and material interwoven with the every day.

ALICEKETTLE.

I first studied Fine Art painting and then went to Goldsmiths College to do a Postgraduate Diploma in Textile Art. My epiphany moment came as I sat at the machines with the realisation that thread had the potential to transport me anywhere and need have no function. I discovered the expressive potential of thread to describe my inner imaginary world and its relationship with the world outside in all its guises. I found that with stitch you can construct, draw and examine the inside and outside, back and front of living. I discovered how to deal with the loss of my mother not through a sentimental response but as a reflection of the deep rooted interests she had in textile and craft. It was a time when I was desperately searching for life to have meaning and purpose. I clung onto a line of thread and have carried on doing so ever since.

I just like sewing, I like the transformative conversations of cloth and thread which personifies the substance and material of life, the narrative of the local and the epic, the historical and the continuity of making.

I first joined the 62 Group in 1986 but pressure of work caused me to leave after five years, I was invited back as a Honorary Member in 2009. It felt like the return of the prodigal.

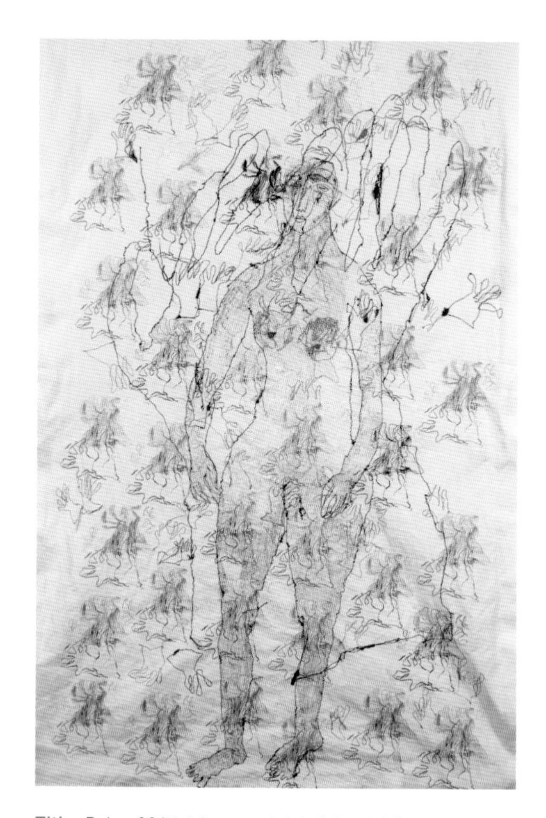

Title: Ruko, 2011 (above and detail far right)
Size: 131 x 226 cm
Materials: machine stitch, digital stitch
Photo: Joe Low

Title: Mio, 2011 (detail right)
Size: 131 x 226 cm
Materials: machine stitch, digital stitch
Photo: Joe Low

When I was a child it was at a time when Japan was not a rich country, so my family did not enjoy an easy life, so we had to be creative and make our own clothes and other household items, but we were happy and enjoyed ourselves. Perhaps it was this aspect of my childhood that led me towards my eventual artistic career.

Being a young Japanese lady, I was expected (like my peers) to master the traditional Japanese arts, which included Shibori (tie dye) and embroidery. When, later in my life I had the opportunity to renew my studies I travelled to the UK to study traditional (western) methods of embroidery at Goldsmiths College and it was here that I was encouraged to discover the freedom of expression I needed to further develop my techniques, and to carry on my studies at the Royal College of Art.

SHIZUKO KIMURA.

Since the western concept of 'life drawing' does not exist in Japan, my work might seem to the, casual, viewer to reference western traditions and possibly they would not be aware that I also trained in embroidery in Japan. I see myself as working in a form of figurative fine art, but it is important to me that the viewer does recognise that my work does have a textile root.

I joined the 62 Group in 1998 and have noticed that, since then, conceptual and abstract works have become more prominent. For the future I would like to see a greater involvement of the Group in education at school and college level.

Title: Models in New York II (detail).
Size: 2.5 x 1.14 metres
Materials: cotton muslin. Silk, cotton and synthetic threads
Photos: Junichi Kanzaki

Title: Origami
Size: 1.1 x 0.9 metres
Materials: cotton muslin. Silk, cotton and synthetic threads
Photos: Junichi Kanzaki

I was born in Halifax, and all my family, in some way, worked in the textile industry. My grandmother, who was a professional embroiderer in her early working life, taught me her craft when I was five. I made my first garment on my mother's treadle sewing machine when I was seven. These experiences, together with the introduction to textiles as an art form by my art teacher at school, Vicky Watling, influenced my decision to become involved in textiles. Originally I took a degree in textiles/fashion and then worked as the embroidery designer in the London haute couture house, Bellville Sassoon.

PADDYKILLER.

Over the years, my work has taken various directions, led by commission and exhibition briefs, personal research, and autobiographical events. I have explored architecture, horticulture, the human body, music, my cats, but it is only recently that I have been looking at textiles as a source of inspiration. Although my textile roots are very important to me, and I have, for a long time, been perceived as a textile artist through the use of the sewing machine; arthritis now restricts me, so I have had to adapt my work to processes I can employ. I now enjoy embracing drawing onto other media, such as glass and ceramics, and the use of digital media.

I joined the 62 Group in 1985 and since that time it has expanded the boundaries of textiles to include contemporary media, and ideas. It also encourages both contemporary artists and the general public to enjoy, accept and value textile as an art form at the same level as painting or sculpture.

Title: Walled In (right)
Size: 55.5 x 55.5 x 7.5 cm
Materials: drawing in indian ink on silk, gesso; bonding onto reclaimed bricks
Photo: Paddy Killer

Title: Pose(ur)s through the Looking Glass (below, top)
Size: 100 x 130 x 17 cm
Materials: drawing & painting on silk, mixed media
Photo: Paddy Killer

Title: Great-Great-Uncle Abraham's Blues Collection (below, bottom)
Size: 80 x 60 cm
Materials: drawing, painting & machine embroidery on silk
Photo: Paddy Killer

SECOND FLOOR PLANS
FIREESCAPE PLANS
KENSINGTON HOUSE
APARTMENT
68
YOU ARE HERE

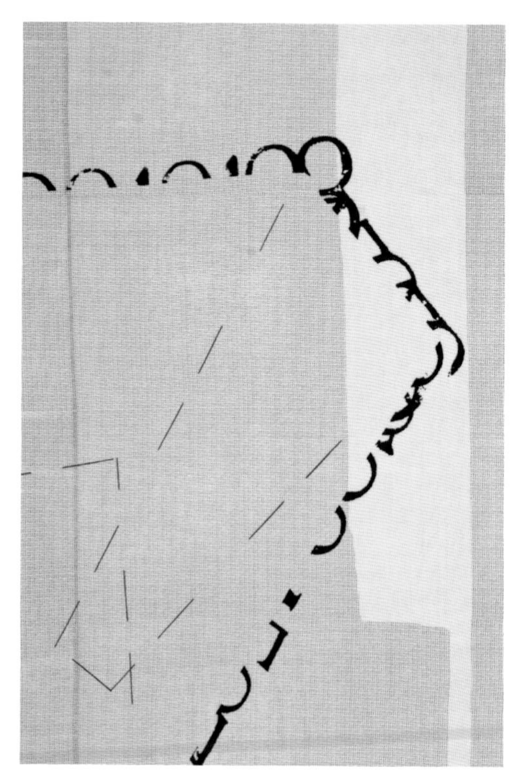

I watched my grandmother make clothes; I was fascinated by her tailor's dummy with its various adjustable wheels and dials. It seemed magical that a delicate brown paper pattern with its different printed symbols – like a secret code that only she understood – could ultimately be transformed into a wearable garment. The methodical process of laying out the pattern, the 'crunching' sound as the sharp scissors cut out the shapes from brightly patterned silks, pinning and tacking together the pieces to create a whole – all this must have had an impact on me. In due course I would embark on sewing projects of my own, excited at the prospect of being able make and wear something in a day – it was a means of personal expression, but with a practical edge.

These early memories didn't consciously make me think 'I want to go into textiles', but made sense when I began my art education.

JOANNA KINNERSLY-TAYLOR.

My degree course was very technical and early on I remember how frustrated I felt with all the weighing, measuring and note-taking that 'got in the way' of being creative. In time I saw the value of this knowledge, as it provided a sound foundation to build on and gave meaning to experimentation and development.

At my core is the need to capture the essence of the everyday through my one-off works. From this source I describe myself as a 'textile artist and designer', as I feel this best defines the scope of my print practice, which embraces several different areas. Although there are no fixed boundaries, I suppose I subconsciously adopt an appropriate mindset for each situation, whilst allowing interesting overlaps to occur. My textile roots don't necessarily extend to the content of my work, though there may be references that evolve from them, remaining 'below the surface', like a quiet foundation.

I joined the 62 Group in 1997 and since then the scope of work has broadened considerably. There has been an increase in members who make more three-dimensional, sculptural works that perhaps use little in the way of textile materials, for example. We have embraced change and become more professional in how we present ourselves to the world.

Title: The Shape of Things (detail, above)
Size: 1.33 x 2.6 metres
Materials: screen-printed Irish linen with reactive dyes and discharge
Photo: Electric Egg Ltd

Title: Lost and Found (right)
Size: 1.34 x 2.0 metres
Materials: dyed and screen-printed wool with reactive dyes, discharge and pigment
Photo: Ruth Clark

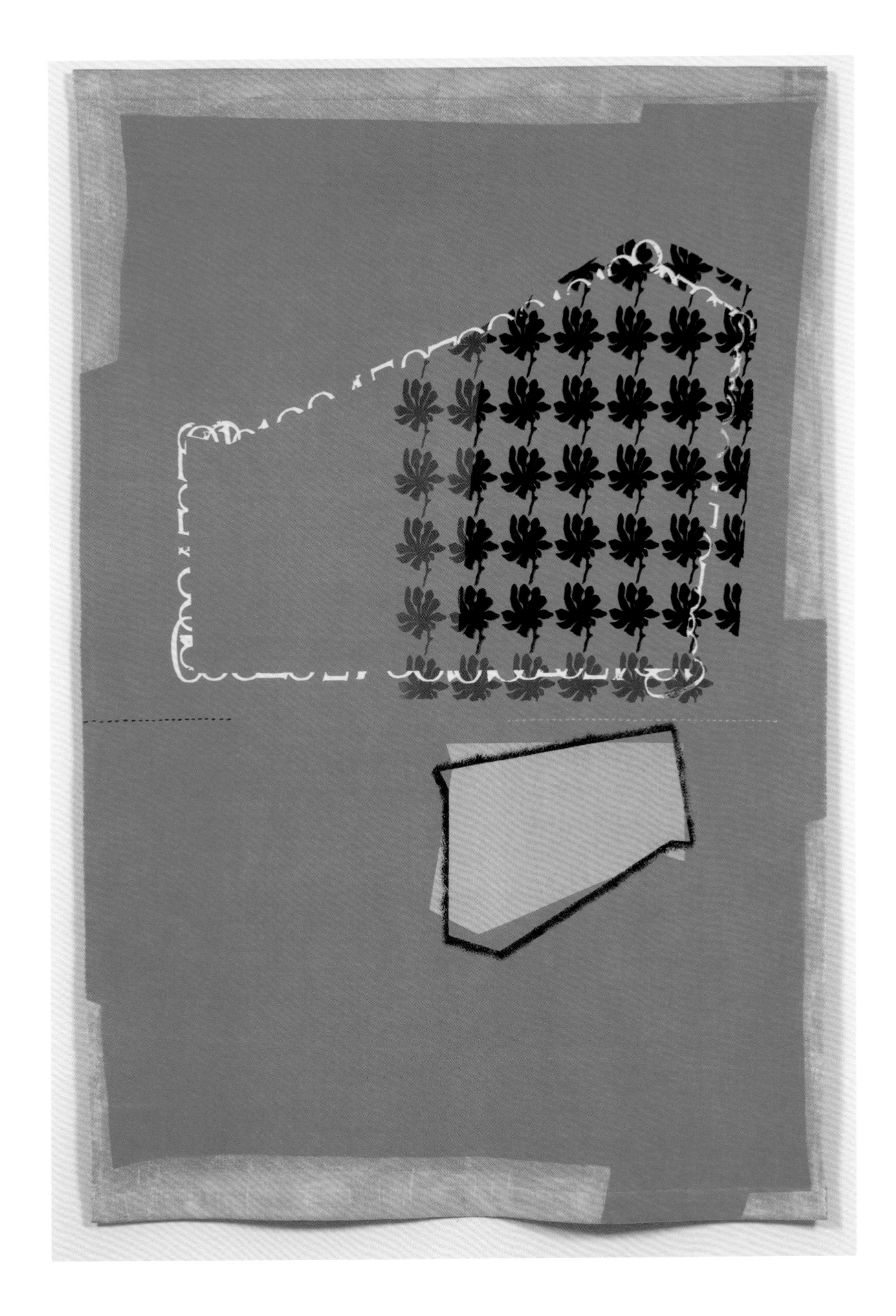

The importance of sewing and making at home had a huge impact on my choice to be involved in textiles. I was brought up to expect to make things and this included not just clothes but furnishings and the construction of simple furniture. I was taught to sew by my grandmother and made dolls clothes from the age of four and simple skirts at eight. I had my first sewing machine in my early teens, a manual Singer machine. The resourcefulness that this background encouraged has been enormously helpful in my textile practice.

JEAN LITTLEJOHN.

I trained in print and surface pattern and my work still references rhythms and patterns. I have an ongoing fascination for ancient textiles, particularly those that demonstrate resourceful responses to the environment such as primitive dwellings, simple cloths, woven bowls. I am particularly interested in how inventive people were with limited materials available to them. My work has taken me to some amazing places and I try to seek out artefacts of ancient peoples, such as basket makers in Alaska, Canada and New Zealand. The way fibres were constructed or joined together is hugely inspirational to me. Traditional kelim carpets have also been a passion. They represent the lives and societies of the people who worked them and walked on them, retracing the footsteps of our ancestors.

In my work I seek to refer to layers of history and the notion that our knowledge is sketchy, often depending on chance findings. There is so much left to discover, history is full of gaps and holes, much like lace, another source of inspiration.

I have been a member of the 62 Group since 1980. It encourages thoughtful and innovative approaches to the use of textiles in contemporary art practice. It also offers a platform for the expression of ideas to those who may not have access to wider audiences without the support and profile of the Group.

Title: In Fragile Footsteps: study (right)
Size: 30 x 40 cm
Materials: Dyed silk chiffon, devore velvet and lace worked on soluble support
Photo: Michael Wicks

Title: Retrace and Reveal: study (below)
Size: 25 x 35 cm
Materials: distressed handmade paper and velvet
Photo: Michael Wicks

My mother always embroidered and still does today at the age of 93. She was trained as a professional seamstress and made all my clothes as a child. As a teenager I tried to continue this skill but I was never very good. Without fail, each garment I attempted, would need major surgery to rectify a big mistake, perhaps in the cutting out of the pattern or the sewing of the garment. But all those years of handling cloth and selecting fabrics left an indelible impression on me, so the decision to become involved with textiles later in my life, can be seen as a natural progression in my work.

JAEMARIES.

Originally I trained as an oil painter but gave up serious painting when babies arrived. The memories of working with cloth and thread returned when I enrolled on a canvas work class. Although I hated every minute of it, finding it too restrictive, I again felt the attraction of working with needles and threads. I moved into appliqué, enjoying the tactile quality of fabrics and then decided to expand my horizons by taking a Diploma in Creative Embroidery.

My ultimate goal has always been to combine cloth and paint. It took me about 10 years to successfully unite these two contrasting techniques. A defining moment arrived while I was working with batik. I realised that I preferred the accidental splashes, brush marks and blobs that occurred spontaneously on the edge of the work, so I tore and ripped out the most interesting areas using them to develop the work in a much more intuitive way – less structured and more fluid. This method of working opened up the possibility of getting back into paint as I began to 'construct' a piece of work, developing layers by patching and piecing fabric areas and combining them with painted areas.

I became a member of the 62 Group of Textile Artists in 1990 and have watched with interest the expansion in the diversity of the members' practice. I believe that it is important that the Group keeps its identity within the field of textiles and this variety of disciplines contributes to the Group's strength and appeal.

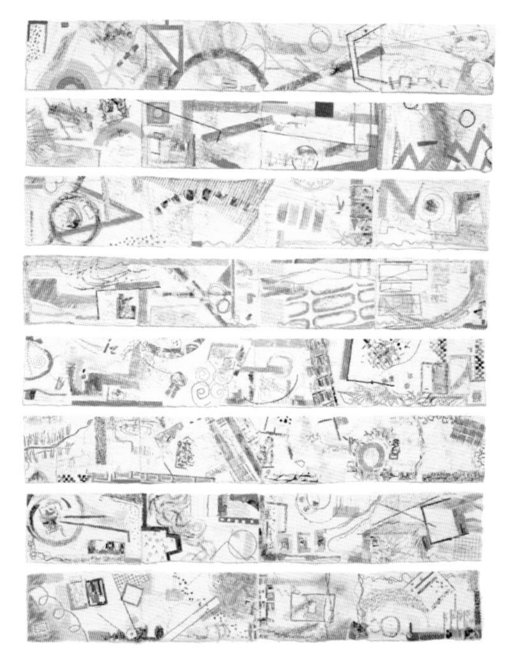

Title: Timelines
Size: 123 x 154 cm
Materials: calico, commercial and hand-dyed fabrics, paper, threads, string, plastics, oil paint
Photo: Michael Wicks

My mother was a strong influence on my decision to become involved in textiles. She was always sewing both domestic items and embroidered pieces either for exhibition or as commissioned pieces, often ecclesiastical. My parents taught at the art college in Swansea and our family activities often revolved around their art projects. Every autumn, the dining room turned into a conveyor belt of us all adding dabs of colour to the black and white greetings cards originally created as wood cuts, scraperboard and lino cuts by my parents. I remember as a child joining a class of my mother's 'grown-up' students at art college where I embroidered some striped cloth and made it into a draw-string bag (I still have it!).

SIÂNMARTIN.

I graduated from Birmingham College of Art with a degree in Embroidery. Although it was an important factor in my development and allowed me to become more spontaneous and look at things in less predictive ways, I am not sure that this training is reflected in my current work. The textile processes in my work reflect those of the past. I am keen to establish a connection between my own work and those who work more traditionally, a language that is common even though individual words might be different.

My work shows my interest in manipulating materials, exploring qualities that allow me to find ways to express simple ideas. My work celebrates the way the material can be stretched for its own sake as well as to make a personal statement. I feel that my work relates to a more materials-based area of contemporary practice rather than perhaps a more expressive one, although I am using the materials to tell their own quiet story.

In 1962, this was the first and only group of its kind and led the way for quite a while until other groups formed. I joined in 1974 and since then the work of the 62 Group has moved from being mainly stitch based to include unconventional materials and to welcome non-stitch practitioners. I hope the Group will continue to take risks and provide a platform for new ideas.

Title: Lifeline
Size: 0.3 x 1.05 x 0.3 metres
Materials: vellum, printed paper, waxed threads
Photo: Stephen Yates

I remember sewing at home with my mother, making embroidered binca mats and stitched kits. I loved making lines of decorative stitching, inventing new stitches and combining stitches in complicated ways. This kept me occupied for hours, totally absorbing me. I remember decorating the hem of my Brownie apron for my needlework badge, and sewing tulips in chain stitch on a cloth in school needlework, it took me a whole school year, but I still have the apron and the cloth.

JANE McKEATING.

Although working with textiles was not discussed as a serious career option as I grew up, I decided to study textiles, mainly because I lacked the confidence to stick my neck out, so I followed what seemed the route for girls from my college at the time. I looked at endless colleges and none seemed quite right, but then I found Goldsmiths, where a student said it was OK just to draw, so I thought 'this is the place for me!' I finally discovered a love for textiles in my final term, so went on to do an MA in Manchester.

The work I do is very illustrative and figurative, but I really like my work to be handled and touched which is not really very practical. I am exploring ways to address this and probably haven't resolved it yet. I have quite recently understood that it's the touch of cloth and stitch in combination with the visual qualities that together communicate something. I like the way that the fingers as well as the eyes can understand the work, it connects up to the process of making itself. Someone once said in a very loud voice at an exhibition of my work, 'why doesn't she just paint?' and I thought about it and knew that I wanted to make it more evident why. Nothing is more beautiful to me than when image, stitch and cloth combine.

I have been making textiles for nearly 30 years now but only joined the 62 Group in 2010. I see the ethos of the Group as being tough, serious, ambitious, with a commitment to quality.

Title: While I was gone - a counting book (above)
Size: whole book 50cm x 20 cm
Materials: digital print and hand embroidery on linen
Photo: Mary Stark

Title: No particular value, transition - pages from rag book (right)
Size: whole book 50cm x 20 cm
Materials: digital print and hand embroidery on linen
Photo: Mary Stark

I think textiles and making skills have always been part of my life and therefore my memory goes back as far as I can remember! In early childhood I grew up in an era where my mother made out of necessity: our clothes, fresh cotton summer dresses, and knitted everything – from jumpers to socks, I think I even recall knitted swimming costumes. She also made her own textiles for the home, and things were repaired not replaced. I was always aware of this tradition of being able to make as being passed on from previous generations. My grandmother was known to be a fine seamstress and hand embroidered linen hankies - a sort of cottage industry.

ELAINE MEGAHEY.

I think the tradition of making had an impact on the choice I made when going to art college. Studying textiles felt like familiar territory. I remember going to see the end of year student shows (1980) and being totally inspired by work in the embroidery department. I recognised certain processes and approaches, but was intrigued by work that pushed the boundaries away from the purely decorative and functional.

I don't necessarily describe myself as a textile artist. I see myself as an artist who employs different processes to express their concerns. Initially, I was drawn to samplers, patchwork and quilt making techniques and the idea of piecing and layering, and the importance of a simple running stitch within the construction. The idea that individuals might stitch in notes or fragments in the making of the quilts also appealed to me with regards to communicating individual and collective stories. This still has some bearing on my work, but there has been a gradual shift over the last 15 years towards working with non-textile processes: drawing, printmaking, photography as well as working with thread/stitch.

I joined the Group in 1989, wanting to be part of a bigger network of artists, which provided a professional platform through which I could show work nationally and internationally. It was about being connected. In recent years there has been a push towards challenging members within the Group to broaden their response in terms of collective exhibitions/ themes. Not always easy to respond to, but it may help to present more unified shows, and in doing so continue to support the Group's longevity and relevance.

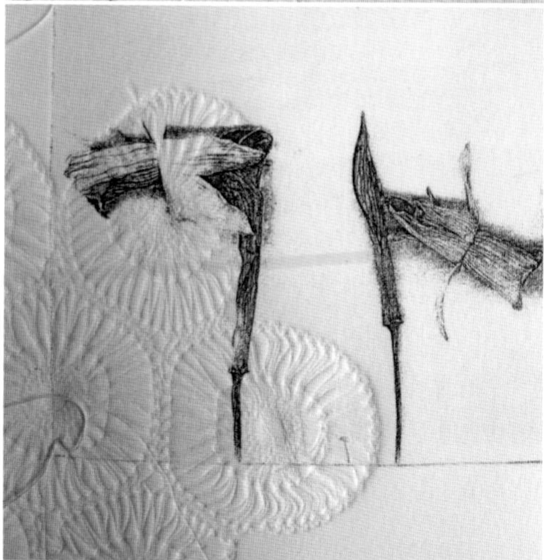

Title: Artists Book (detail, top)
Size: 46 x 60 x 4 cm
Materials: solar plate etching on Somerset paper, letterpress text and linen thread
Photo: Elaine Megahey

Title: Artists Book (detail, above)
Size: 46 x 60 x 4 cm
Materials: Solar plate etching, linen thread, embossing
Photo: Elaine Megahey

Title: Trace-Quiet Shifts, Artists Book (right)
Size: 46 x 60 x 4 cm
Materials: Solar plate etching, linen thread, embossing
Photo: Elaine Megahey

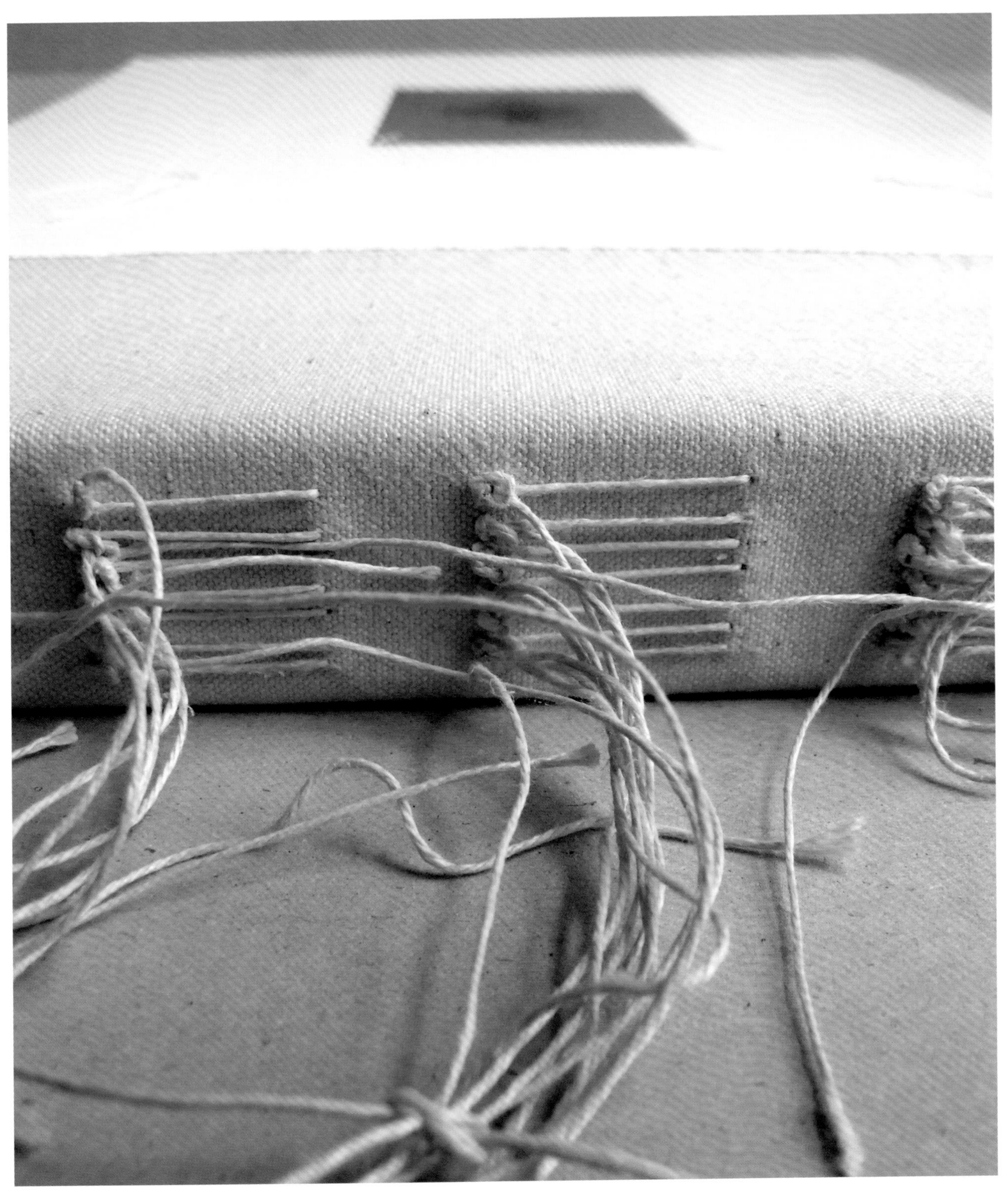

At home, sewing and making were intertwined with mum's memories of her sister's dressmaking business. Young heads were filled with often-repeated family stories of gatherings, 'occasions', relatives, neighbours and places. Narratives woven together so tightly, embellished and layered with details, which we had never experienced ourselves, but that had embedded single words and phrases to invoke the story. My well-remembered 'new' skirt for school was made by mum from a wool fabric – grey/green, thick, stiff and unbending in such a short length and with an unsettling diagonal – which today I recognise was once a cavalry twill overcoat. Unremarkable and unlovely. Except that is for the addition of a pocket shaped like a flowerpot and with lazy-daisy flowers on it. The embroidery was similar to that worked on my shoe bag. I was shown how a single loop could be joined from within to another and another and another to make a chain. When would I be able to make my stitches flow in such a smooth even line? Mum had changed something ordinary into something very special.

JAN MILLER.

The blanket chest in the hall held a store of collected fabric lengths: cotton's from Lewis's, flannelette from Wales, tweed from Scotland, silk from an uncle in India. Each had secured its place by circumstances of its history. Each was periodically considered for use – and rejected as 'not quite right' – but this home handling collection showed that whilst colour and pattern were subjective, touch and feel were essential to make a successful finished garment. Shopping continues to be characterized by how textiles feel and hang – whether in Liberty's, Top Shop or a local market, it is always a tactile experience.

After science teaching in London and work as an editor for an educational publishers, we moved as a family to Norwich. I joined a traditional embroidery course run by an ex Royal School of Needlework student and one day a week for three years stitched meticulously and historically. Bliss! This was the start of my present involvement with textiles.

I joined the 62 Group in 2005 and found it a group that selects and celebrates individuality with high standards, embracing all definitions of textile art without compromise.

Title: Work registers (top left)
Size: 15 x 30 x 20 cm
Materials: paper, linen, screenprints
Photo: Jan Miller

Title: Work light (top right)
Size: 55 x 45 x 2.5 cm
Materials: parchment, monofilament, acetate, glass
Photo: Jan Miller

Title: Work place (detail right)
Size: 55 x 45 x 2.5 cm
Materials: parchment, monofilament, shards, perspex
Photo: Jan Miller

In my mid-forties I enjoyed rearing a flock of rare breed sheep and breeding golden retrievers, my sons were teenagers and I enjoyed playing golf which I have had to give up due to a neck injury. I found I had time on my hands, so I joined a local sewing group and found I was enjoying it so much that I wanted to discover more and enrolled on the following courses. City & Guilds studies part 1 and Level 3 Diploma in Design and Craft both with Opus School of Textile Art, Regent's College London. I discovered with surprise how much creativity I have and how this flair soon became an addiction.

MARY-ANNE MORRISON.

My work has evolved from the studies I worked with on the courses. Using a sewing machine enables me to create and formulate three-dimensional textile sculptures made up of multiples using my own technique. Manipulating different mediums in the most unexpected ways regenerates me to build a new body of work. I like to challenge materials and bring opposites together e.g. controlled and uncontrolled; measured and accidental, and complete the challenge with a balanced form.

I was delighted to join the 62 Group in 2006 because it is the leading textile group maintaining the highest standards in textiles, pushes the boundaries and is an example to aspiring artists.

Title: Abacus (detail, far right)
Size: 35 x 51 cm
Materials: organza bias binding outlined with stitch
Photo: Michael Wicks

Title: Peelings (above right)
Size: 135 x 35 cm
Materials: coloured thread
Photo: Michael Wicks

Title: Peelings (detail, right)
Size: 135 x 35 cm
Materials: coloured thread
Photo: Michael Wicks

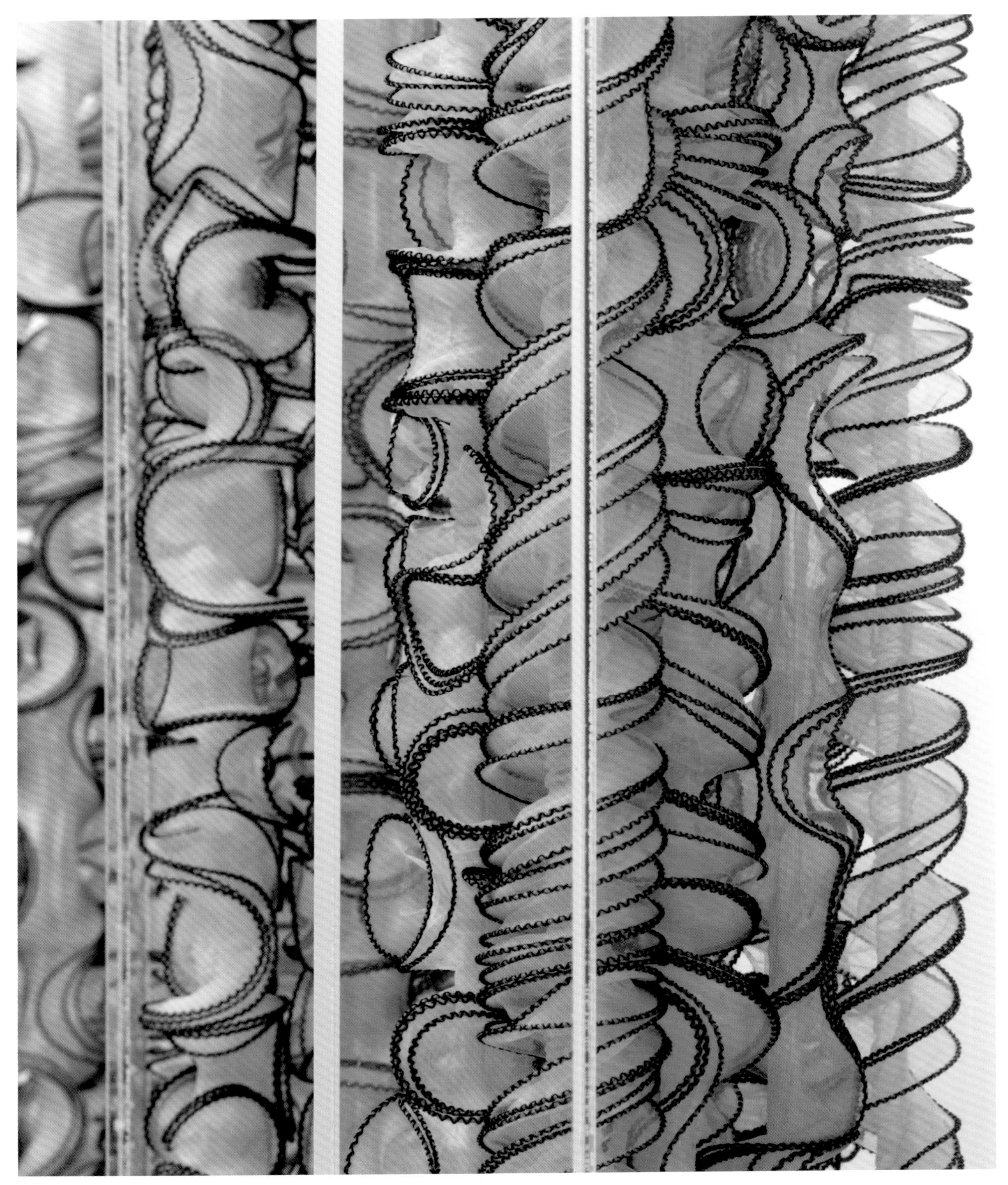

I remember embroidering a horse on an old hessian feed sack while still a child on our Sussex smallholding – I was about 6 years old at the time. In later childhood my favourite game was 'making things' out of old cereal packets, tin cans and feed sacks etc, and I often tied or stitched these materials together. These days I've substituted slate for card but I'd say that what I'm doing now is pretty much a continuation and development of my childhood games.

Title: Kirkby Roundhead
Size: 44 x 60 x 1 cm
Materials: Kirkby Moor slate, linen and sisal thread.
Photos: Lucy Barden

CLYDE OLLIVER.

Although I love textiles (kilims, servicemens' wool pictures, traditional knitting etc) none of these practices feature in my own work. Rather I'm more influenced by artists such as Richard Long, David Nash and Andy Goldsworthy than by any textile practitioners, past or present. For me, the material suggests the work, so the finding of slate or other stone is a pivotal part of the process.

Although my current work doesn't reference my textile training, I do feel all my work does have some sort of textile root, even the carved stone reliefs and drawings, but it is not important to me that the viewer recognises this. Nowadays I don't really see myself as a 'textile artist' as such, though much of my work has sufficient textile elements (stitch) for it to qualify for textile shows and inclusion in the 62 Group.

I joined the 62 Group in 2009 and hope that it will continue as an exhibiting group while giving much more attention to questioning our relationships with curators, academics, the art world etc. As artists/makers most of our time is taken up with the process of making, not with exhibiting, and the Group could do worse than devote proportionally more time to addressing issues arising from practice.

My mother did not indulge in garment stitching, however she did make exquisite beaded handbags, and I had aunts on my paternal and maternal sides, who were professional dressmakers. They designed and executed entire bridal ensembles, even making the silk flower bouquets. In my native country Sri Lanka, at that time ready-made clothes were not freely available. Furthermore, sari blouses were stitched to individual body measurements in order to create closely sculpted garments. It was simultaneously exciting but frustrating to be surrounded by the most talented seamstresses producing such beautiful pieces of stitchery. So at the age 10 I scavenged all the scraps of fabric leftover from my aunts' dressmaking orders and made a patchwork quilt. And at the age of twelve I attended Singer Scientific Dressmaking classes and acquired the skills to stitch for my mother and myself.

SUMI PERERA.

I originally studied for an MBBS in Medicine, then a MSc in Virology, followed by a PhD in Virology. However, even whilst working as a doctor and scientist, I had continued trying my hand at a spectrum of activities including textiles, pottery, blacksmithing and glass blowing. When my scientific research group moved to Scotland, I decided not to follow, providing an ideal opportunity for a career change and to focus more on my artistic practice. I began making and selling artworks, which involved textile assemblages. Despite enjoying textiles as a craft-form, I wanted to explore the role of textiles in the fine arts. Therefore, when I began my MA, textiles and cloth featured very heavily in my work, alongside the full range of printmaking techniques from the traditional (etching, screenprinting, collagraph etc.) to digital methods. My textile roots are important since I now work full time as a multi-disciplinary book artist and have given up practicing as a doctor and scientist. However, my work is heavily influenced by my medical background.

I joined the 62 Group in 2008 and hope it continues to push the boundaries of textile art, perhaps collaborate with other collective art groups, and encourage multi-disciplinary exchange and activities.

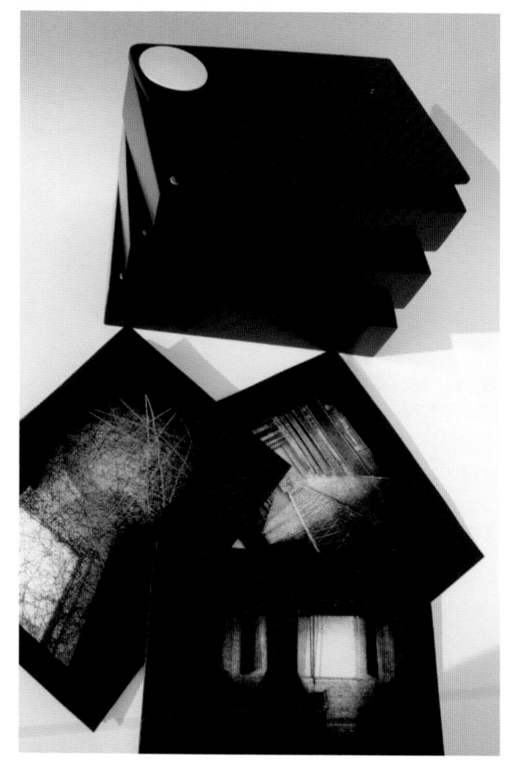

Title: Climbing The Sticky Ladder III [6th Kyoto Hanga, Japan] (far right)
Size: 58.5 x 13 cm
Materials: etching, aquatint on somerset paper with stitch
Photo: Sumi Perera

Title: Wire in the Blood (work in progress, right)
Size: 15 x 24 cm (each module)
Materials: knitted copper wire within fused glass
Photo: Sumi Perera

Title: Shattering The Glass Ceiling IX [Freud Museum] (above)
Size: 10 x 15 cm (each)
Materials: etching, aquatint on somerset paper with stitch
Photo: Sumi Perera

Title: Perception III [Helen Keller Award] (above right)
Size: 15 X 21 cm
Materials: etching, aquatint on somerset paper with stitch
Photo: Sumi Perera

My mother made her own clothes, altered clothes (added collars, shortened hems, took in darts); repaired clothes (darned elbows, patched holes in sheets); and my grandmother knitted (and taught me). As a young girl, when my mum was making an item of clothing she would let me have some of the scrap material to play with. I liked cutting it up with her pinking shears. The pieces would get smaller and smaller until it was too small to cut. Occasionally, I'd try to make a piece of clothing for one of my dolls. I don't ever remember being successful but I do remember having a go.

MARILYN RATHBONE.

This had an impact on my decision to become involved in textiles because it made me comfortable with textile materials. I took my degree in Fine Art and gradually moved into textiles. I didn't really decide to, it just happened. By the time I graduated, I was working predominantly in textiles and two of my Pavement Works pieces were selected for Art Textiles 2 · the second major survey of British artists working with textiles. Although, at this time, I still considered myself to be an artist who only sometimes uses textiles in her art, in hindsight, I realise that even then I'd begun to 'think' in textiles.

It's the more 'humble' textile practices that inspire me. Since joining the 62 Group, my interest in the overlooked or ordinary has continued and I've revisited two techniques that I've used from time to time in box making: inkle weaving (straps) and braid making (lid stays). I've also continued to experiment with a variety of wrapping and binding techniques (previously used for Pavement pieces) for example: button making.

My work is minimalist, my goal to blend concept and content as simply as possible. Sometimes, my research uncovers an underlying political, social or historical issue and, when it does, the issue may become the focus of the piece. At other times humour plays a part.

When I joined the 62 Group in 2002, curators were very keen to have themed 62 Group exhibitions but recently have been more relaxed about themes and more interested in promoting the diversity within the Group.

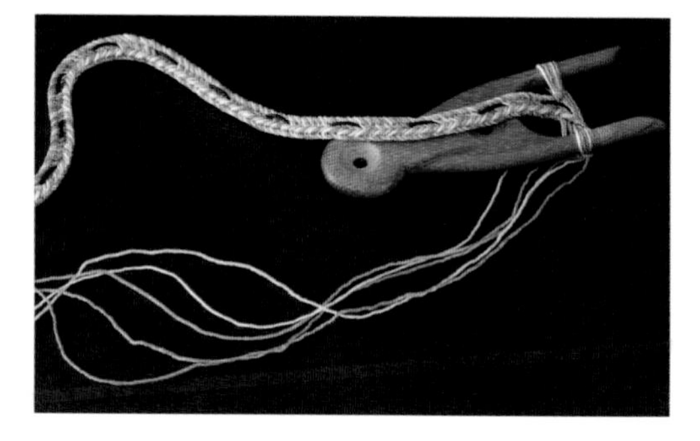

Title: Equivalent IX · Set out the coloured counters at a tangent to one another to form different shapes and patterns. (above right)
Size: 10 x 11.1 x 11.3 cm (boxed) 3.3 x 0.7 cm (each counter)
Materials: brass curtain rings, hand-dyed silk thread, information booklet, handmade box
Photo: Marilyn Rathbone

Title: 100 Metres Dash: My dream is to complete a 100 metres dash. With a lot of hard work, and if I braid as well as I can, in 2012 I hope to achieve that dream. Details of work in progress (above and below right)
Size: 10,000 x 0.7 x 0.5 cm (when finished)
Materials: hand-dyed, hand-braided silk thread; book and dvd of the event with personal training program, regular updates and progress chart.
Photo: Marilyn Rathbone

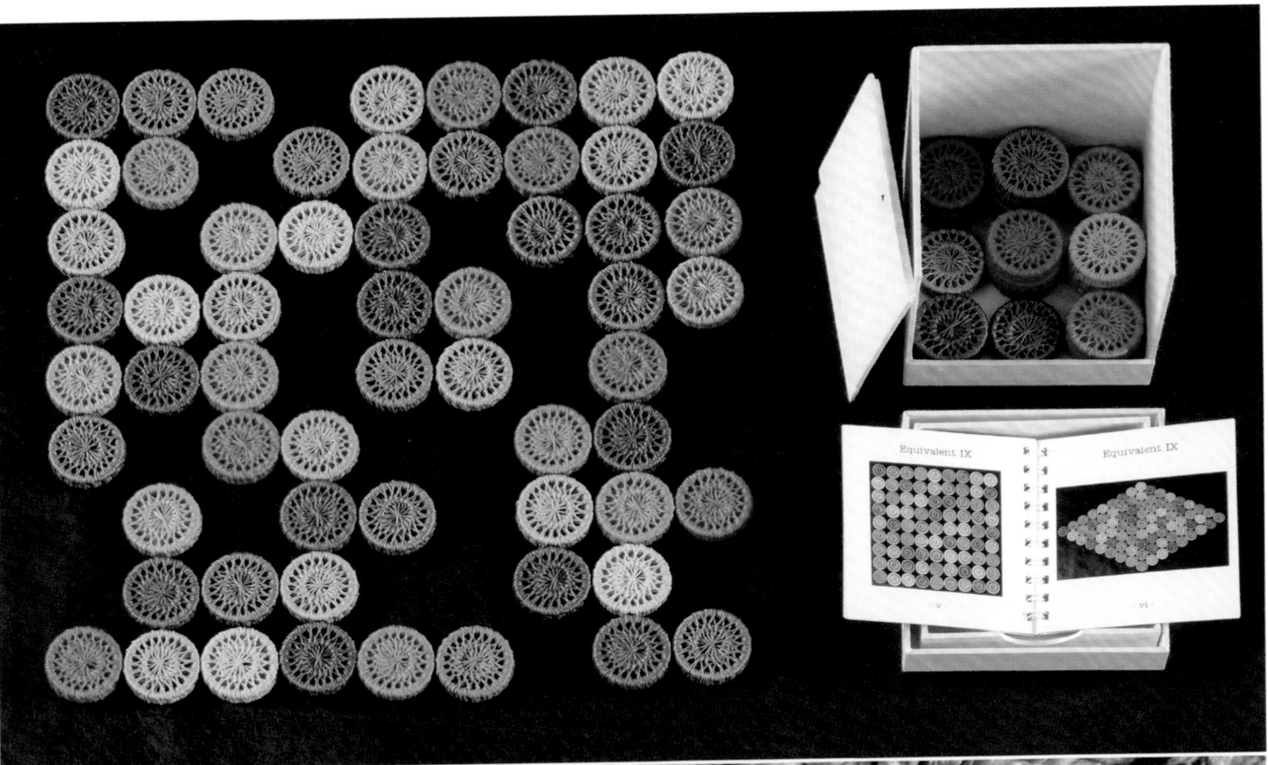
Equivalent IX
Equivalent IX

When I was a child my parents said they were going to see my Scottish grandmother. I busily made a comb case for them to take up to her the next day. That night I heard my father saying on the phone that his mother had just died and that he had to go to Scotland – nothing was said to me. After they had gone I found my comb case still in my mother's dressing table drawer. When they returned I was told how much my grandmother had loved my comb case. From that day onwards I always worried whether my other grandmother was alive or dead if I didn't frequently hear from her.

SHUNARENDEL.

The experience has made me be honest about truth however disturbing.

After sculpture training at St Martins under Anthony Caro my journey into my current practice began on holiday in Wales when the children were young. I became interested in natural dyeing, collected wool from fences, collected plants and mordants, dyed the fleece, learnt to spin, learnt to weave, found cloth weaving too flat for me, tried tapestry weaving, extended into 3D, met Myriam Gilby and loved the freedom and sculptural possibilities. A Diploma in Constructed Textiles led me to 3D pieces developed from netted techniques and eventually into flexible forms using basketry materials. My work has continued to reference this training – I see it more and more as 3D drawing in space. Analysing structures, testing the reaction of materials on them, exploding them, seeing how far a structure can be pushed, metaphorically, in any direction, and trying to understand the 'engineering' and stresses and strains so as to create form from an unstable structure.

I joined the 62 Group in 1993 and hope that in the future we will continue to encourage daring and thought-provoking work of a high standard whether this be of a conceptual, political, aesthetic, or technological nature. I am in favour of collaborations with other disciplines. Textile is important, but the work (outcome) is the most important and if the root is strong enough it will always shine through.

Title: Pleated Rhythm (top and detail far right)
Size: 70 x 30 x 27 cm
Materials: dyed chair cane
Photo: Stephen Yates

Title: Break, break, break on thy cold gray stones, O Sea (right and detail above)
Size: 2.25 x 0.65 x 1.25 metres
Materials: dyed chair cane, monofilament and wire
Photo: Sandy Rendel

Weaving is about as traditional as it gets and it is a discipline.

In the early 70's I was a student on holiday in Crete. At that time weaving was still being done by the women in their village homes. I watched fascinated as a black clad woman sat at her simple wooden loom in a whitewashed house. She was weaving a length of brightly coloured cloth and all was peaceful save for the clacking movement of the loom. The wool yarn was rough and tightly spun and was being woven into the traditional Cretan bags used by the men and women. We had no common language but there was a communion in her weaving. I went back the next day and she had finished the cloth and made me a bag that is used and treasured to this day. Weaving was to be my future from that day.

FIONA RUTHERFORD.

In 1976 I saw the exhibition Sacred Circles at the Hayward Gallery, which celebrated 2000 years of North American Indian art and it was my introduction to Navaho weaving. I was blown away by their power and skill. This is what I wanted to do. Peter Collingwood was also a huge influence. He shared his knowledge and love of weaving so generously and his book The Techniques of Rug Weaving was my starting point and guide. I first started weaving on a small home-made frame, moving to weaving rugs on a floor loom and then to tapestry weaving as my designs became more abstract and fluid. These textile roots are my starting point and anchor – where I've come from and where I'm going to. My recent work is about the human history held in cloth; the stories that lie in the threads of remnants, patches and selvedges. There is an ancient and universal bond in weave.

I joined the 62 Group in 1997 to be part of a textile network and to meet the people whose work I so admired. My hope is that the Group continues to champion 'textiles' and all that that means. Its strong sense of identity should continue to be a source of inspiration for young artists and a challenge to a sceptical art world.

Title: Haiku 1,2,3
Size: 34 x 34 cm each
Materials: woven cotton, linen and sewing thread
Photo: David Lawson

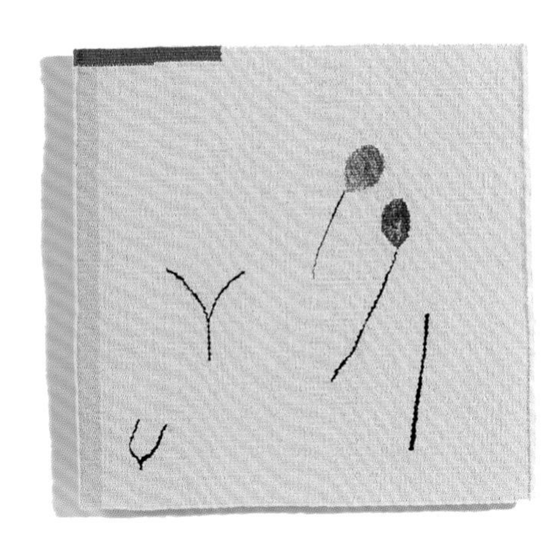
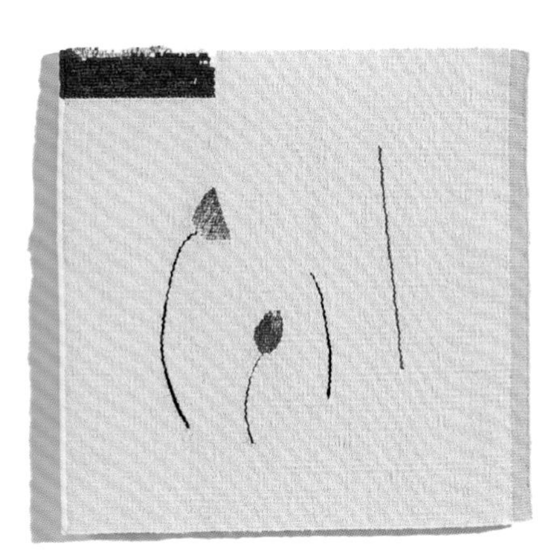

I love textiles: the material and the technique have always been with me. I like the feel and touch of it. For me textiles are not just a medium but do tell their own story and are very suitable to communicate emotions.

I started to stitch when I was probably 5 or 6 years old. My mother used to stitch pillowcases and tablecloths and that had quite an influence in my being interested in using that technique. My mother trained me basic stitching and that is what I still do. But I have developed it a bit, I suppose. Especially the way I now use couching is not much seen around. I am interested in traditional samplers and I expect that the viewer would see the influence of this tradition in my work.

TILLEKE SCHWARZ.

I had an art training, mainly focused on free style drawing. In the sixties I was very impressed with the Pop Art movement and enjoyed the freedom in working in this way. Many people – nowadays – also recognise a relationship to graffiti.

My main interest is the content of my work. Actually, all my works are part of a continuing story, a personal reflection on modern life. I include anything that moves, amazes or intrigues me. This results in a subtle comment on our modern society. I hardly need to use my imagination because 'real life is often more strange than fantasy'. My main muse is a beautiful Norwegian forest cat.

I have been a member of the 62 Group since 2005 and my hope for the future is that the Group will continue to develop its international connections and keep using textiles as their main medium.

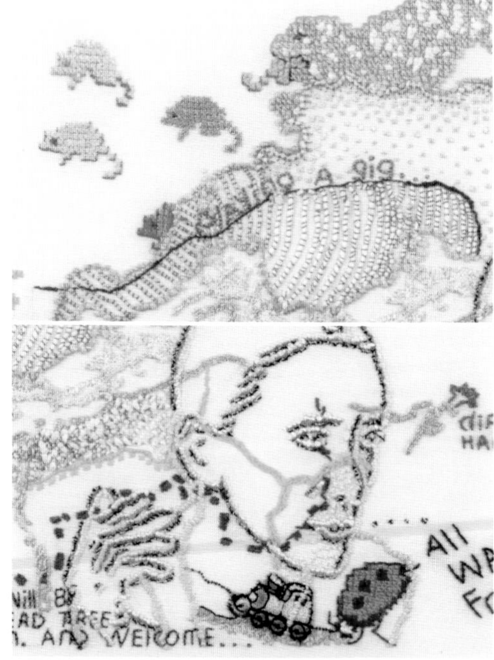

Title: Free recovery, 2010 (right and details above)
Size: 68 x 66 cm
Materials: hand embroidery on linen
Photo: Rob Mostert

FREE RECOVERY
DRESS CODE
UNAUTHORISED DISCLOSURE OF THIS AND/OR ANY IS STRICTLY FORBIDDEN.
FREE RECOVERY
AWAIT RESCUE
FREE RESCUE!
AWAIT RECOVERY
SEA SCAPE
HAVE NOT GIVEN UP ON INTERNET DATING
TILLEKE SCHWARZ THE NETHERLANDS
FORGOT YOUR PASSWORD?
REMOTELY DETECTED
CLYDE, DE CAT HAD A N EMOTIONAL REUNION WITH
OWNER.
THINK
WHAT DO YOU THAT CO ULD BE IMPROVED
SELECT THE TOPIC
HOW CAN YOU HELP?
FOGGY
DEAR GUESTS, BREAKFAST IS A OW SERVED BETWE EN 7:15-8:15 am on WEEKDAYS. THANK YOU MR. TOM BOLA
PROUD TO BE A BRITISH
KITTENS SURVIVED A FULL WASHING MACHINE CYCLE
WAY TOO WORDY
RETURN TO LOG
CLIFF HANGER
ALL WAITING FOR
THE CAKE STALL WILL BE GINGERBREAD FREE AFTER 9 AM. AND WELCOME...
SOMETIMES WE TWIT
A BIT WACKY
IS THIS GIRL TELLING ALL HER LIFE?
IN LIEU OF FLOWERS
RESERVED!

I went to art college and studied textiles under Audrey Walker at Goldsmiths. I was going to do an academic subject but having been to art school parties they seemed much more fun, I was quite open minded on foundation but really loved working in textiles and colour and so went down that route. I did mostly tapestry and embroidery at college but with embroidery I saw it as something women from other cultures knew about and so it had more connections. I am interested in the history of textiles too and love the universal nature of cloth.

LYNN SETTERINGTON.

I contextualise my work within the textiles/art arena, but I don't see myself as a real craftsman, the idea is much more important then my finish and making skills. Generally I work by hand which is slow and time consuming, but I love the intimacy of working that way and the engagement with the physicality of materials. Everyone rushes around nowadays so there is a calmness to working by hand that I relish. Contemporary life and representing the overlooked, be it people, objects or rituals are key concerns, folk art too has always been an important touchstone in my work. My current body of work is concerned with signature, more especially handsewn cloths and quilts. These are artifacts made from 1850's onwards, all commemorating the sewn signatures of ordinary people. In creating new cloths, I am exploring social networking old and new and investigating collaborative work with a wide range of groups.

I joined the 62 Group to allow me more opportunities to show my textile work also to meet people interested in similar concerns. I have been a member for 2 years but was a member for 5 years back in the 1980's. I see the ethos of the Group as promoting and expanding textiles to a broader audience. The future will, I hope continue the good work, educating and informing the broader public to the scope of textiles and to help raise the status of a lot of overlooked artists.

Title: My Signatures (above and detail)
Size: 1.05 x 1.05 metres
Materials: cotton fabric and threads computerised machine embroidery and hand quilting
Photo: Stephen Yates

Title: Mums are Heroes (right)
Size: 1.65 x 1.90 metres
Materials: cotton fabric and threads, hand embroidered
Photo: Stephen Yates

Safeway
www.Safeway.co.uk
Somerfield
Raising money to
TESCO
M
MORRISONS
More reasons to shop at Morrisons
PLEASE RE-USE THIS BAG AND HELP TO PROTECT THE ENVIRONMENT
Iceland
...because
Mums are heroes!
Quality Foods
co op
The Community Retailer
www.coop.co.uk
Customer Careline 0845 7000100
are you standing
next to one?
our mystery shoppers
ensure you're getting the best...
Sainsbury's
making life taste better
ASDA
Price
Always LOW PRICES
www.asda.com
KWIK SAVE
100% Degradable
www.kwiksave.co.uk

I was first introduced to felt making in a school art class where I produced a very basic square of felt. I remember that it was a eureka moment and from that time on I was completely hooked. Unfortunately then art was not seen as a 'proper' subject and like many other students I was channelled into academic study, in my case, languages. Years later after a career and a family, I had the luxury of being able to return to college and study art. For my foundation course I specialised in textiles, in particular felt making. I realised then that this was my path and the start of an incredible journey, exploring, creating and challenging.

SUZY SHACKLETON.

Like many felt artists I am very aware of the history of felt making and the deep roots it has in the culture of communities. I have studied the traditional techniques of wet felting, inlays, mosaics etc however parity between old and new is important to me. I like to take both traditional and modern methods and blend it with my contemporary style to create illustrative vibrant pieces.

I live and work in the hills of the beautiful Peak District so all around me is ever changing inspiration but also I am challenged by techniques, to find and use unique methods to create that certain line, shape or tone. I am influenced by exciting textures, bold designs, and quirky compositions but most of all I am a colourist. The context for my work is where I stand now as an artist and at the moment I am firmly rooted in the art of traditional felt making yet stretching and moulding my work into ever new directions.

I joined the 62 Group in 2008 and so I'm relatively new to the Group. I became a member because the Group was recommended to me as a community of textile excellence and I aspired to be part of that community so that my own personal practice would be raised and assessed through exhibition selection processes etc. I think the future direction of the Group should continue to be growth; expanding minds, creative practices and skills but always outwards and in all directions.

Title: Gossips in the Greenhouse (above)
Size: 108 x 85 cm
Materials: felt
Photo: David Shackleton

Title: Greenfinch (right)
Size: 91 x 74 cm
Materials: felt
Photo: David Shackleton

I remember making simple dolls clothes with my mum when I was little and decorating them with hand stitching. She also taught me and my sister to knit when we were quite small. When she was younger she used to decorate tablecloths with embroidery and drawn-thread work. There were always a lot of fabrics and threads in the house and I had a grandmother who was a dressmaker.

KAYSMITH.

I wouldn't say these early experiences had a direct influence but maybe subconsciously. I always enjoyed crafts and think that was probably because of my mum but it was just an interest and I didn`t consider it could lead to an art course or employment. However I eventually studied Design Crafts where I first learned, and fell in love with, weaving, and then completed an MA in Textile Culture.

I love the long tradition of weaving and the suggestion that by weaving (and encouraging others towards weaving), I am a part of continuing that tradition. Weaving permeates so many avenues from technology, cultural traditions, language and mythology which for me, enriches the craft.
I love the idea that threads can become fabric through the simple act of interweaving and that the way we weave today is not that far removed from some earlier looms.

I hope the textile references in my work are obvious, because textiles is what I do, so even if the work evolved as film, photography or drawing, textiles is always the basis or root, for that work. A few years ago I did a workshop on Peruvian backstrap weaving during which we looked at the importance and significance of weaving within the Peruvian culture, for example how it relates to procreation and a woman's position within society. I later made a piece of work inspired by this and considered the idea of a bundle of heddles as being representative of a living, beating heart which related to both Peruvian and British culture.

I joined the 62 Group in 2007 and have found support and encouragement to develop practice and take textiles in whatever direction you choose, whether textile, film, installation, photography, audio etc.

Title: Spider writing, spider weaving (detail, right)
Size: 268 x 13.5 cm
Materials: cotton yarn
Photo: Gillian Tapping

Title: Silent writing, silent weaving (detail, far right)
Size: 268 x 13.5 cm
Materials: cotton yarn
Photo: Gillian Tapping

Title: Drawing of Woven Cloth (below)
Size: 22.5 x 22.5 cm
Materials: pen on card
Photo: Gillian Tapping

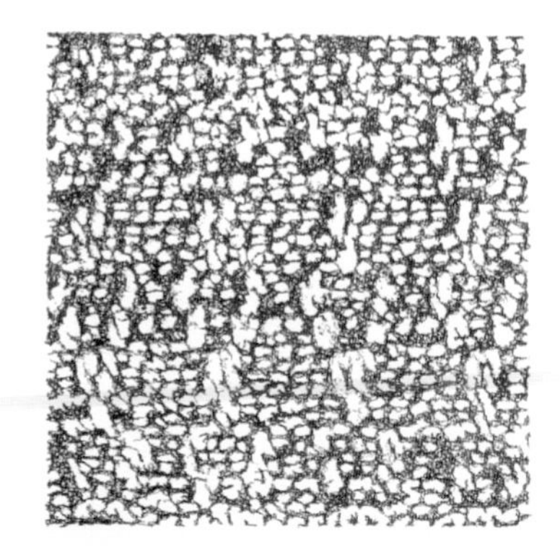

Title: Weave II (detail, right centre)
Size: 51.5 x 17 cm
Materials: pins and cotton thread
Photo: Gillian Tapping

Title: Weave II (detail, right)
Size: 51.5 x 17 cm
Materials: pins
Photo: Gillian Tapping

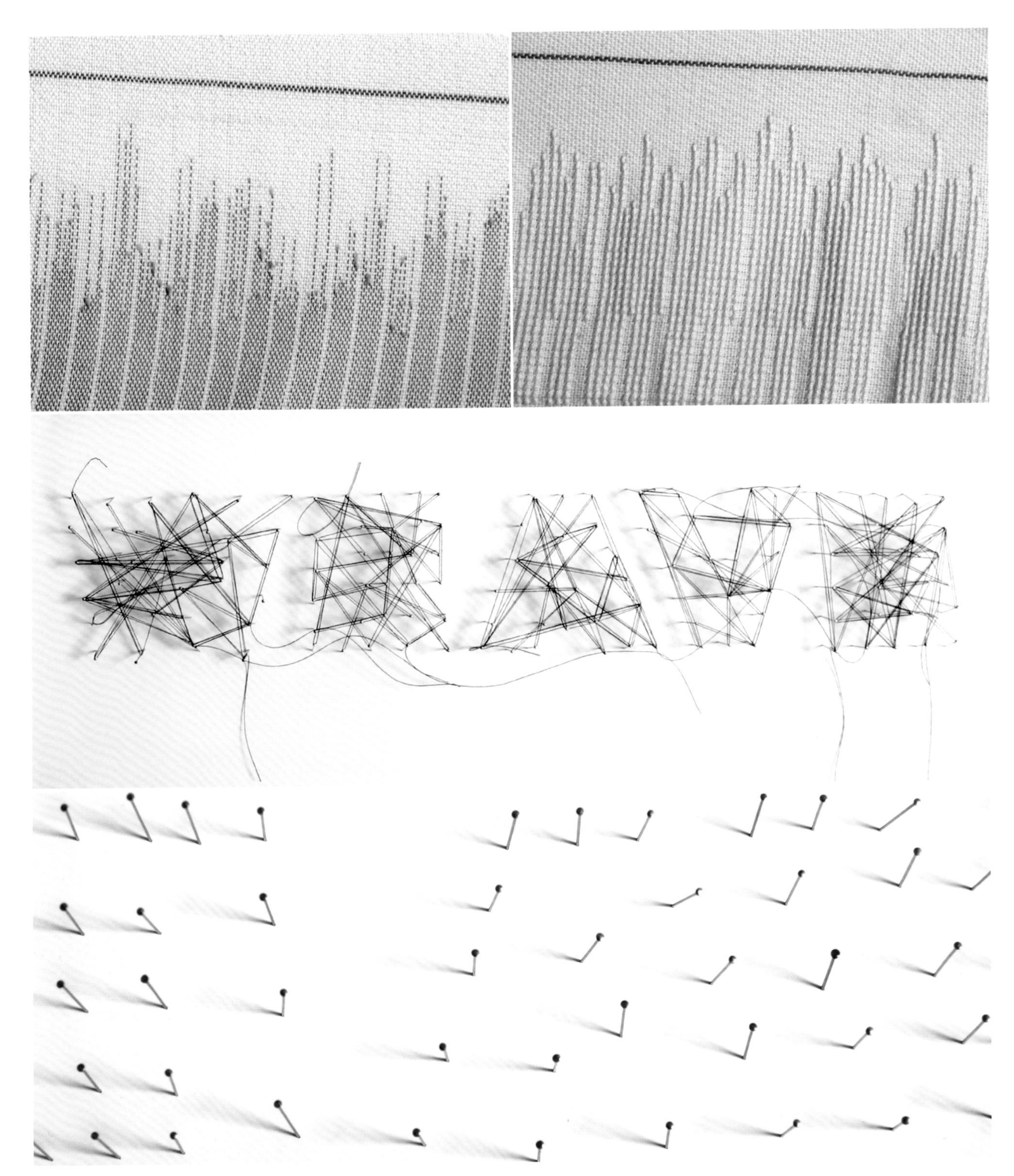

I come from a very creative background; strangely almost everyone can sew, basic day-to-day alterations and on more technical levels; my mum always has an ongoing project, appliqué quilts or samplers; in his younger years my dad repaired the sails on his round the world yacht race; my brother works for Aardman as an animator, and has made his own characters from fabric in the past.

AIMEESPILSTED.

Textiles was a natural move for me in the final year of my Contemporary Craft degree, having also experimented with wood, metal, and ceramics. Initial learning stages encompassed most traditional methods: weaving, Shibori, appliqué, felt making, and devore were a few. My current work most certainly references my textile training, and I am very proud to be a textile artist. I especially love the tactile and ambiguous nature of fabric and also being able to take apart pieces and start over; building layers with pieces that have already had so much time invested in them, I think it's a beautiful process.

My work was initially inspired by Venice, and the distilled sense of history, time passed and the preserved buildings; it has now expanded to include urban and rural landscapes, boatyards and the Wirral Coastline. I have also been influenced by National Museums Liverpool's amazing collection of archived worldwide textiles. Photography features strongly throughout, to catalogue textures, subtle colour changes, and layering. Techniques and samples are processed to simulate and mimic the initial qualities recorded from site visits. Each piece makes its own choices, developing organically and will often be de-constructed and re-constructed.

I have been a member of the 62 Group for 4 years and enjoy the shared passion with the Group for increasing awareness of contemporary textiles and the urge to stretch the boundaries of fabric and stitch.

Title: Red Thread Runs
Size: 52 x 75 cm
Materials: driftwood, leather, suede, waxed cotton, linen, corduroy, sail fabric, jacket lining, paint, varnish, fishing twine, tent attachments, and other found flotsam pieces
Photo: Paul Goonoo

Title: Red Thread Runs (reverse side, below)
Size: 26 x 41 cm
Materials: leather, suede, waxed cotton, linen, corduroy, sail fabric, jacket lining, paint, varnish and fishing twine
Photo: Paul Goonoo

My mum was a tailoress so I learned to sew at a very early age. I started designing and making clothes, first for my dolls and later for myself. Although I didn't like dressmaking, I loved the challenge of designing and pattern cutting. My school didn't place much importance on Art, certainly not as a career choice so on leaving school I went to work as a laboratory assistant. Luckily a friend suggested I should apply for the art foundation course. My mum encouraged me to apply to St Martins School of Art and she was absolutely thrilled when I was offered a place to study there. I suppose looking back on it now I was fulfilling her own dream of becoming a designer. She had always designed her own clothes and also clothes for her two daughters but did not have the opportunity for further education having left school at fourteen.

SUESTONE.

When I first moved to London to study, one of our first projects involved drawing the costume and textile collections at the Victoria and Albert Museum. I was totally blown away by the experience and it probably contributed to my transference from fashion design and into a more fine art approach to textiles, although it took me a few years and a move to Goldsmiths College to realise that. I loved stitching and, although, I went on to design womenswear for 28 years, I was always determined to come back to it. I love the whole feel of manipulating cloth and using thread as a means of mark making. My work is mainly figurative and regionalist and the skills I use, whilst having a lot in common with drawing, promote stitching as laudable discipline in its own right.

I first joined the 62 Group in 1975 but had to leave due to outside pressures. In 2008 I re-applied and was delighted to be accepted by a group with such a good reputation whose standards are so high. My hope for the future of the Group is to embrace the new without ever losing sight of how we got there.

Title: Family with Fish 2011 (below and details, right)
Size: 76 x 125 cm
Materials: hand and machine stitched textile: recycled cotton, linen and silk clothing and hand dyed fabrics with cotton threads
Photos: Steve Thornton, www.thorntonconnect.com

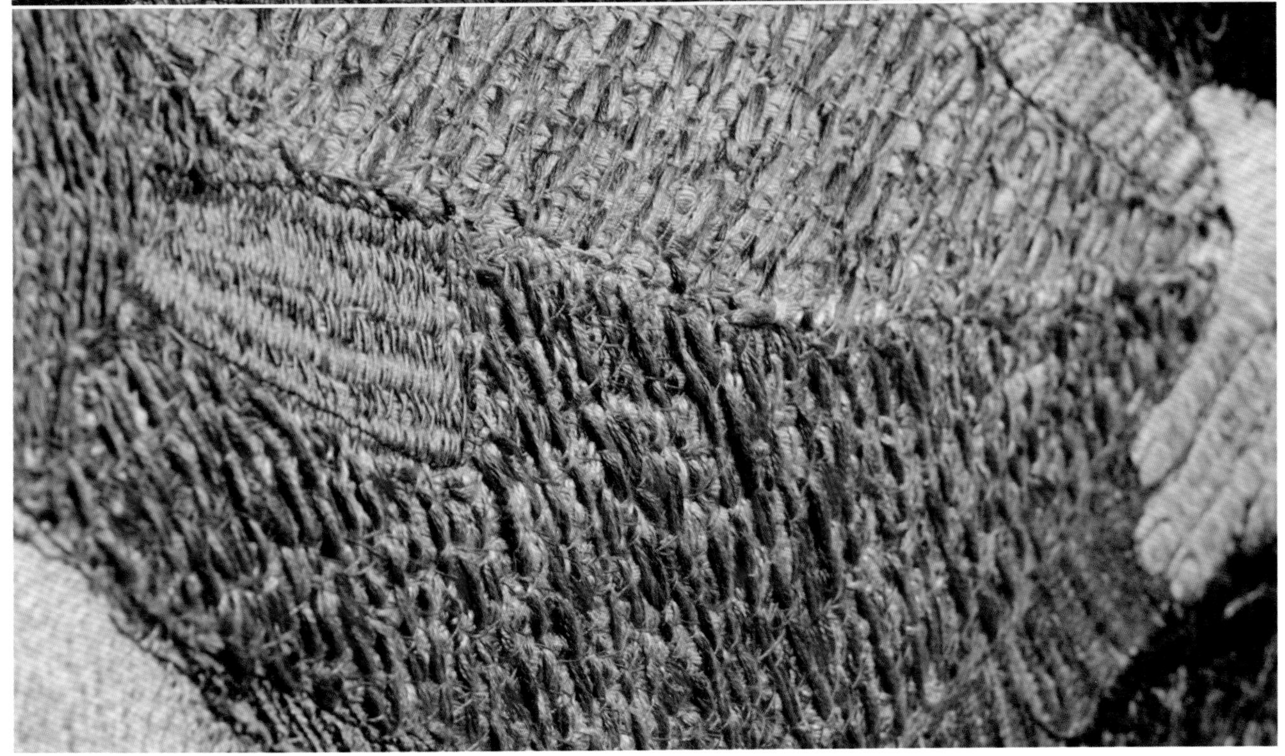

Title: Restoration 1
Size: circa 15 metres
Materials: repaired tree with stitches
Photos: Hannah Streefkerk

My mother taught young children textile techniques and my sisters and I had also to learn the different techniques for at least one hour a day after dinner. At that time I did not like that too much – knitting drove me crazy – but I always loved embroidery.

HANNAHSTREEFKERK.

Although I did not like the evening lessons (I think because they were compulsory) I now know that it helped me a lot. At the Art Academy I studied interdisciplinary arts, with no textiles; however a few years after I finished studying I had an exhibition in which I wanted to create something soft and kitsch. I started to embroider a pillow with a picture of two kissing people (the installation was about love) While embroidering that pillow I felt so good, it almost felt like coming home. Since then my work has radically changed. I started to create nature inspired embroidery. I always loved nature and landscape very much and textile techniques and landscape are for me almost the same.

I thanked my mother a lot, because of her and that daily hour (!) it is easy for me to use many techniques (but I still hate knitting...)

For me it is important to show my vision and concept in my work and mainly I use crochet and stitch because the results of these techniques are precisely how I want things to look. The 'stitch' is very important to me. This one small element connects things, can repair, can hold things on their place and that is very interesting to me. That such a small element has so much to say, has so many strength in it. Just the act of making a stitch is for me a wonderful mark.

I joined the 62 Group in 2006 and would like it to become more international. And to keep up the high quality! Somehow I would like to know all the members better and better, so that more ideas can be shared and discussed. Sometimes I miss the opportunity to this, and joining a group means for me this.

I love hand stitching: the intimacy with the material and quietude it conveys. The 'alchemy' of dyeing fabric and paper with indigo also inspires me.

ELIZABETHTARR.

In my first year at Goldsmiths College, some 30 years ago, I realised that if you can get a needle through it (or drill a hole to enable this) you can stitch it! We were trained thoroughly in all the textile techniques: hand and machine stitch, weaving, dyeing, screen-printing, felt making. We were also exposed to contemporary makers in textiles. This grounding in techniques has enabled me to make art with confidence.

My art practice is based on ideas: having something to say, a story to tell. Techniques and materials are important but secondary, and it is not important to me that a viewer recognises my work as having a textile root.

A college mate encouraged me to join the 62 Group over 20 years ago – she said it would pay off – and she was probably right! The Group aims at excellence in textile art practice, pushing boundaries, and there's an educational slant as well. I'd like the 62 Group to step out of the 'textiles' definition in our future exhibitions.

Title: Infanta Series: Run (right)
Size: 80 x 48 cm
Materials: paper, fabric, indigo, paint, stitch
Photo: Michael Wicks

Title: And Three Trees on a Low Sky (below and detail))
Size: 36 x 36 cm
Materials: paper, fabric, indigo, paint, stitch
Photo: Michael Wicks

Title: Alcyone (ii) (below and detail, right)
Size: 55 x 95 cm
Materials: fabrics and threads
Photo: Michael Wicks

As a child in the 1930's in the north of England, I was part of a proud working class family where it was assumed that the women MADE everything to improve their circumstances. They sewed or knitted new clothes and patched or darned old ones: they 'prodded' rugs, they embroidered cushions and pillowcases and, in my mother's case, embroidered silk pictures for 'the front room'. I was urged to learn these skills in readiness for an assumed future as wife and mother. I wasn't interested — I was dreaming of 'something else'.

AUDREY WALKER.

Fortunately I was awarded scholarships which took me to art schools to study painting. It never occurred to me that embroidery might be taken seriously as an art form. Then, by chance in 1960 I saw an exhibition of 'fabric collages' by Margaret Kaye — I was entranced ! Painting was set on one side as I plunged into new possibilities. Instinctively, I turned to one of the simplest skills -sewing by hand or machine. I explored areas in museums which I had previously ignored, discovering textile works which carried strong meanings in diverse cultures across centuries. BUT, where was the contemporary work in Britain? It seemed to be invisible. Then I discovered the 62 Group, artist led and determined to break through the barriers which stood in the way of exhibitions of embroidery in good public venues. I was accepted as a member in 1967.

Over the years the Group has grown and the work has evolved and diversified . We have a strong 'core' to our work with roots in a marvellously rich textile heritage. This is our identity and strength as we look forward to new challenges and possibilities ahead.

I came to textiles very much on my own which I think is unusual, I didn't have any stories/memories of textiles whilst growing up. However, I do remember making a set of curtains with my mother for the first flat I bought. This was well after my MA in Textiles and at that point I already worked teaching textiles and had my own studio practice. Of course, I had read the theoretical texts surrounding domesticity, making and story telling which had never really touched a cord before. But, I suddenly had this experience of sitting with my mother, chatting and stitching. It was a really lovely experience, and it was only later that I realised I'd had an experience of textiles that I'd only read about previously!

HELENWESTON.

I do not fit easily into a particular discipline, the work treads a line between textile and metal, fine art and craft. I have found that it is a difficult line to tread in relation to galleries and exhibitions. I think people looking at my work would be surprised that I trained as an industrial woven textile designer and now make sculptural objects out of sheet metal incorporating various textile techniques. But it is evident to me. How I approach and think about the construction of my sculptures is driven by my interest in woven construction. Although it may not be obvious in my work it is very important that I approach it from a textile root, for various reasons both personal and professional. I always find solace in handling material, and it is this that keeps me making work. I play with a mixture of themes, touching on autobiographical traces to make multiple series of works. The combination of textile elements and processes with metal work references a domestic and decorative aesthetic and juxtaposes it with a utilitarian feel.

Since joining the 62 Group in 2003 it has been alert to the shifts within textiles, fine art and art practice as a whole, and been open to artists using different mediums that might conceptually challenge the notion of what 'textile' can be and mean. I want the Group to celebrate its achievements, consolidate its history and be flexible within a shifting landscape.

Title: Stack, 2009
Size: 26 x 75 x 26 cm
Materials: cotton gimp thread, foam sheet, sheet aluminium, sheet brass, sheet copper, perforated stainless sheet, oak
Photo: Ivan Coleman

When I was a child, every evening I would sleep on the pretty embroidered pillowcases my mother made for me. Whilst in nursery, I made myself an embroidered bag decorated with chestnuts especially for a nut-picking excursion with the class. My grandfather ran a children's clothing company so I always wore embroidered, smocked, appliqué or knitted good quality clothes and also silk kimono for learning Japanese dance. The embellishment of cloth was like air for me.

ATSUKO YAMAMOTO.

When I was 25 years old I decided to pursue a career in embroidery and textile art. I studied traditional Japanese embroidery which was very important; I learned the patience to finish the work, which seemed endless. All my time was taken up in embroidery and in thinking about art and design. Not only did I study the technique, but I studied the traditional colours used, the patterns, shapes, design and material. I also gained an insight into the hidden spiritual world of Japanese art & craft.

I am interested in Origami because the two-dimensional becomes three-dimensional purely through the action of folding a paper, and Mariano Fortuny is my greatest influence as he made clothes only through folding. Through his influence I started experimenting with pleats – the way the action of folding can make the material bounce or stretch. I decided to make three-dimensional objects from pleated cloth. These became installations, a space of meditation, which reflects back to the Origami which, although it is just a folded paper contains spiritual meanings.

Although I treasure my background – embroidery most of all, I do not use textile materials and it is not important for the viewer to recognize the textile roots of my work. It is more important that the viewer appreciates my work from their own sense, feeling and experience.

I joined the 62 Group in 1984 and I want always to be a member! Over the years the Group has grown and developed, encompassing traditional techniques, assemblage and conceptual concerns. The Group maintains their identity and high standards through rigorous discussion of each piece submitted.

Title: Crystal Jungle (right)
Size: installation
Materials: silk, cotton
Photo: Yutaka Suzuki

Title: Justice 20 (left)
Size: installation 18 x 2.5 metres
Materials: silk, feathers
Photo: Yutaka Suzuki

EXHIBITING MEMBERS

HONORARY MEMBERS (EXHIBITING)

HONORARY MEMBERS (NON EXHIBITING)

Morag Gilbert
Jennifer Gray
Margaret Hall-Townley
Jennifer Harris
June Hill
Jan King
Janet Ledsham
Alison Liley (Mrs Erridge)
Barbara Marriott
Professor Lesley Millar MBE
Professor Anne Morrell
Linda Parry
Hannah Frew Paterson MBE DA
Sue Prichard
Andrew Salmon
Diana Springall
Barbara Taylor

FRIENDS

Miranda Brookes
Maria Theresa Fernandez
Heather Martin
Lesley Mitchison
Irene Ord
Barbara Siedlecka
Isabel Wright

HISTORY OF THE 62 GROUP

1962-6	Five annual exhibitions held at the Embroiderers' Guild, Wimpole Street, London (from 1964 these exhibitions toured the UK under the auspices of the Art Exhibitions Bureau (AEB)
1967	Exhibition sent to Australia Exhibition, Royal Festival Hall, London (AEB)
1968	Foyles Art Gallery, Charing Cross Road, London Harrogate Art Gallery (AEB)
1969	Embroiderers' Guild, Wimpole Street, London Victoria and Albert Museum, London Touring: Wolverhampton; Geffrye Museum, London; Boston; Manchester; Stockport; Wandsworth; Lincoln; Walthamstow; Haverfordwest
1970	TUC, Congress House, Great Russell Street, London Inn on the Park, London
1971	National Museum of Wales, Cardiff
1972	Nottingham Library Commonwealth Institute Gallery, London TUC Congress House, Great Russell Street, London **'10 by 10'** **(commemorating the 62 Group's 10th. anniversary)**
1973	Cartwright Hall, Bradford **'Embroidery and Fabric Collage'**
1974	Commonwealth Institute Gallery, London **'Embroiderers at Work'**
1975	National Museum of Wales, Cardiff TUC Congress House, Great Russell Street, London **'Stabiles'**
1976	Metropole Arts Centre, Folkestone Greenwich Theatre Gallery, Greenwich
1977	TUC Congress House, Great Russell Street, London Greenwich Theatre Gallery, Greenwich
1978	Commonwealth Institute Gallery, London **'Textile Artists'**
1979	Woodlands Art Gallery, Greenwich National Museum of Wales, Cardiff
1980	Usher Gallery, Lincoln
1981	Winchester School of Art Gallery, Winchester John Holden Gallery, Manchester
1982	Embroiderers' Guild, Hampton Court Palace **'Signs and Symbols'** **(commemorating the 62 Group's 20th anniversary)** Seven Dials Gallery, Covent Garden, London **'Textile Aspects'**

1983	Victoria Art Gallery, Bath **'Textile Aspects 2'** DLI Museum Gallery, Durham
1984-5	Touring Japan: Tokyo, Kyoto, Osaka
1985	Touring: Clarendon Park, Salisbury (organised by Embroiderers' Guild) Crafts Council Gallery, Belfast; Wexford, Eire; Swansea, Wales; Cheltenham; South Hill Park **'Handspan'**
1986	Swansea University Gallery **'No More Than a Foot'** Stitch Design, Docklands, London **'No More Than a Foot'**
1987	Contemporary Textile Gallery, London * Leicester Museum and Art Gallery **(62 Group's Jubilee Year)** Woodlands Art Gallery, Greenwich
1988	Gawthorpe Hall, Lancashire City Art Gallery, Walsall
1989	Embroiderers' Guild, Hampton Court (New Members) Turnpike Gallery, Leigh * Collins Gallery, University of Strathclyde, Glasgow **'Crossing the Border'**
1990	Bradford Textile Arts Festival, Leeds Polytechnic and Salts Mill, Bradford
1991	Shipley Art Gallery, Gateshead **'Fascinatiing Fibres'** Oxford Gallery, Oxford *
1992	Embroiderers' Guild, Hampton Court **(commemorating The 62 Group's 30th.anniversary)** Touring: University of Ulster, Belfast Collins Gallery, Strathclyde University, Glasgow Commonwealth Institute, London Hankyu Art Gallery, Japan York Festival *
1993	Bankfield Museum and Art Gallery, Halifax Textil Plus, The Netherlands
1994	Royal Cornwall Museum, Truro
1995	Bury Museum and Art Gallery, Lancashire Braintree Museum and Art Gallery, Essex The Black Swan Guild, Frome *
1996	Quarry Bank Mill, Styal, Cheshire
1997	Collins Gallery, University of Strathclyde, Glasgow **'The Language of Touch'** Shire Hall Gallery, Stafford
1998	Drumcroon Arts Centre, Wigan Touring: **'50/50: The Challenge of Restraint'**

The Opera House, Tel Aviv, Israel; Tatton Park, Cheshire;
The Knitting and Stitching Shows at Alexandra Palace, London, Dublin, Harrogate

1999 Maidstone Museum and Art Gallery, Kent **'On and Off the Wall'**
City Centre Art Gallery, Edinburgh

2000 Shipley Gallery, Gateshead **'Out of the Garden'**

2001 Cajobah, Birkenhead
Bankfield Museum, Halifax **'A Collective Response'**

2002 Touring: **'Red'** **(commemorating the 62 Group's 40th anniversary)**
Bury St. Edmunds Art Gallery, Suffolk
Beverley Art Gallery, Yorkshire
Irish Linen Centre and Lisburn Museum, Co. Antrim
Up Front Gallery, Penrith, Cumbria
Midlands Art Centre, Birmingham

Victoria and Albert Museum, London **'In Context'**
Retrospective at the Knitting and stitching Shows, Alexandra Palace, London, Dublin and Harrogate **'In Retrospect'** **40th.Year**

2003 Harley Gallery, Welbeck, Nottinghamshire **'In Place'**

2004 The Millennium Galleries, Sheffield **'Material Evidence'**

2005 University Museum of Zoology, Cambridge **'Encounters'**

2006 Hove Museum and Art Gallery, Sussex **'Tracing Threads'**

2007 Victoria and Albert Museum, London **'COLLECT'**
(8 selected members)
Touring: Textile Gallery, the Knitting and Stitching Show;
Birmingham, London, Dublin, Harrogate

2008 Rochester Art Gallery, Kent **'Size Matters'**
Catmose Gallery, Rutland **'Stuff'**

2009 Touring: The Hub, Sleaford, Lincolnshire **'Bending the Line'**

2010 Tour continuing: Museum Rijswijk, Rijswijk, The Netherlands
Collins Gallery, University of Strathclyde, Glasgow
'Bending More Lines'

2011 Gallery Oldham, Oldham **'At a Tangent'**

2012 Gallery of Costume, Platt Hall, Manchester **'Interventions'**
Holden Gallery, Manchester **'62@50'**
(commemorating the 62 Group's 50th.anniversary)
The Knitting and Stitching Show at Alexandra Palace, London,
RDS Dublin,
Harrogate **'50th Anniversary Package Tour'**

* denotes this gallery invited individual members to exhibit

ISBN 978-0-9571242-0-2

DIRECT DESIGN BOOKS
The Warehouse, Culverden Square, Tunbridge Wells, Kent TN4 9NZ

Published by	Direct Design Books
Editor	Lesley Millar
Line Editor	June Hill
Designer	Gerry Diebel
Publications Assistant	Lily Diebel
Retouching	Alison Wickens
Design & production	www.directdesign.co.uk
Print	www.foxprintservices.co.uk
62 Group logo	www.luminouscreative.co.uk

First printed in 2011

All credits for photographs of artists work are with the images.

The book Radical Thread has been published in December 2011 to celebrate and showcase the work of The 62 Group of Textile Artists.

ACKNOWLEDGEMENTS

The 62 Group wishes to thank our many friends and followers of creative textiles who have encouraged us to publish 'Radical Thread'. We are particularly grateful to Professor Lesley Millar for her editorship and introductory chapter, and to Gerry Diebel for his design work.

Thank you to the University for the Creative Arts for their support of Professor Millar.

We would also like to express our gratitude for the financial support we have received from Madeira UK Ltd. and Coats Crafts UK and for the continuing interest and support for the 62 Group's work from Andrew Salmon of Creative Exhibitions Ltd.